Learning to Love
Data Science

*Explorations of Emerging Technologies and
Platforms for Predictive Analytics,
Machine Learning, Digital Manufacturing,
and Supply Chain Optimization*

Mike Barlow

Beijing · Boston · Farnham · Sebastopol · Tokyo

Learning to Love Data Science

by Mike Barlow

Printed in the United States of America.

Published by O'Reilly Media, Inc., 1005 Gravenstein Highway North, Sebastopol, CA 95472.

O'Reilly books may be purchased for educational, business, or sales promotional use. Online editions are also available for most titles (*http://safaribooksonline.com*). For more information, contact our corporate/institutional sales department: 800-998-9938 or *corporate@oreilly.com*.

Editor: Marie Beaugureau	**Interior Designer:** David Futato
Production Editor: Nicholas Adams	**Cover Designer:** Ellie Volckhausen
Copyeditor: Sharon Wilkey	**Illustrator:** Rebecca Demarest
Proofreader: Sonia Saruba	

November 2015:   First Edition

Revision History for the First Edition
2015-10-26:   First Release

See *http://oreilly.com/catalog/errata.csp?isbn=9781491936580* for release details.

978-1-491-93658-0

[LSI]

For Darlene, Janine, and Paul

Table of Contents

Foreword

I met Mike Barlow a couple of years ago at an industry conference in New York. Our mutual interest in the Industrial Internet of Things (IIoT) has led to many interesting conversations, and I have observed some parallels in our experiences as authors.

We have both written about the convergence of key trends such as big data analytics, digital manufacturing, and high-speed networks. We both believe in the IIoT's potential to create new jobs, open new markets, and usher in a new age of global prosperity.

And both of us are glad he landed on the name *Learning to Love Data Science* for his book. He easily could have named it *How Data Science Is Helping Us Build a Better, Safer, and Cleaner World.*

Mike and I agree that information captured from machines, fleets of vehicles, and factories can be harnessed to drive new levels of efficiency and productivity gains. As much as I love data science, what I love even more is how it can unleash the power of innovation and creativity across product development, manufacturing, maintenance, and asset performance management.

We're not talking about ordinary analytics, like the kind that serve up recommendations when you use a search engine, but the complex physics-based analytics that detect meaningful patterns before they become an unforeseen problem, pitfall, or missed opportunity. This enables us to deliver positive outcomes like predicting service disruptions before they occur, across a wider spectrum of industries, affecting more people in more places than we could have dreamed of even three years ago.

Recently, I've read about how data science and advanced analytics are replacing traditional science. Commentary like, "All you need to do is look at the data," or "The data will tell you everything you need to know," is espoused without really understanding or appreciating what is happening in the background.

Data science isn't "replacing" anything; to the contrary, data science is adding to our appreciation of the world around us. Data science helps us make better decisions in a complex universe. And I cannot imagine a scenario in which the data itself will simply tell you everything you need to know.

In the future, I envision a day in which data science is so thoroughly embedded into our daily routines that it might seem as though the data itself is magically generating useful insights. As Arthur C. Clarke famously observed, "Any sufficiently advanced technology is indistinguishable from magic." Perhaps in the future, data science will indeed seem like magic.

Today, however, heavy lifting of data science is still done by real people. Personally, I believe human beings will always be in the loop, helping us interpret streams of information and finding meaning in the numbers. We will move higher up in the food chain, not be pushed out of the picture by automation. The future of work enhanced by data will enable us to focus on higher-level tasks.

From my perspective, data is a foundational element in a new and exciting era of connected devices, real-time analytics, machine learning, digital manufacturing, synthetic biology, and smart networks. At GE, we're taking a leadership role in driving the IIoT because we truly believe data will become a natural resource that ignites the next industrial revolution and helps humanity by making a positive difference in communities around the world.

How much will the IIoT contribute to the global economic picture? There's a range of estimates. The McKinsey Global Institute (*http://bit.ly/1FfsHAW*) estimates it will generate somewhere between $3.4 trillion and $11.1 trillion annually in economic value by 2025. The World Economic Forum (WEF) predicts it will generate $14.2 trillion in 2030. I think it's safe to say we're on the cusp of something big.

Of course, it involves more than just embracing the next wave of disruptive innovation and technology. The people, processes, and culture around the technology and innovation also have to change. Frankly, the technology part is easy.

Standing up a couple of Hadoop clusters and building a data lake doesn't automatically make your company a data-driven enterprise. Here's a brief list of what you'll really need to think about, understand, and accept:

- How the cultural transformation from analogue to digital impacts people and fundamentally changes how they use data.
- Why it's imperative to deliver contextually relevant insights to people anywhere in the world, precisely when those insights are needed to achieve real business outcomes.
- Creating minimally viable products and getting them to market before your competitors know what you're doing.
- Understanding how real machines work in the real world.
- Rewarding extreme teamwork and incenting risk-takers who know how to create disruptive innovation while staying focused on long-term strategic goals.

The Industrial Internet of Things isn't just about data and analytics. It's about creating a new wave of operational efficiencies that result in smarter cities, zero unplanned outages of power and critical machinery, enormous savings of fuel and energy, and exponentially better management of natural resources. Achieving those goals requires more than just programming skills—you also need domain expertise, business experience, imagination, and the ability to lead. That's when the real magic begins.

This collection of reports will expand your understanding of the opportunities and perils facing us at this particular moment in history. Consider it your head start on a journey of discovery, as we traverse the boundary zone between the past, present, and future.

—*William Ruh,*
Chief Digital Officer,
GE Software

Editor's Note

This book is a collection of reports that Mike Barlow wrote for O'Reilly Media in 2013, 2014, and 2015. The reports focused on topics that are generally associated with data science, machine learning, predictive analytics, and "big data," a term that has largely fallen from favor.

Since Mike is a journalist and not a scientist, he approached the reports from the perspective of a curious outsider. The reports betray his sense of amused detachment, which is probably the right way to approach writing about a field like data science, and his ultimate faith in the value of technology, which seems unjustifiably optimistic.

At any rate, the reports provide valuable snapshots, taken almost randomly, of a field whose scale, scope, and influence are growing steadily. Mike's reports are like dispatches from a battlefield; they aren't history, but they provide an interesting and reasonably accurate picture of life on the front lines.

—Michael Loukides,
Vice President, Content
Strategy, O'Reilly Media

Preface

I first heard the term "data science" in 2011, during a conversation with David Smith of Revolution Analytics. David led me to Drew Conway, whose data science Venn diagram (reproduced with his permission in Figure 1-1) has acquired the legendary status of an ancient rune or hieroglyph.

Like its cousin, "big data," data science is a fuzzy and imprecise term. But it gets the job done, and there's something appealing about appending the word "science" to "data." It takes the sting out of both words. As a bonus, it enables the creation of another wonderful and equally confusing term, "data scientist."

Confusing is the wrong word. Redundant is a better choice. Science is inseparable from data. There is no science without data. Calling someone a "data scientist" is like calling someone a "professional Major League Baseball player." All the players in Major League Baseball are paid to play ball. Therefore, they are professionals, no matter how poorly they perform on any given day at the ballpark.

That said, the term "data scientist" suggests a certain raffish quality. Indeed, the early definitions of data science usually included hacking as a foundational element in the process. Maybe that's why so many writers think the term "data science" is sexy—it conveys a sense of the unorthodox. It requires ingenuity, fearlessness, and deep knowledge of arcane rituals. Like big data, it's shrouded in mystery.

That's exactly the sort of thinking that gets writers excited and drives editors crazy. Imprecise definitions aside, there's an audience for stories about data science. That's the reason why books like this one are published: They feed our need for understanding something that seems important and yet resists easy explanations.

I certainly hope you find the contents of this book interesting, entertaining, and educational. This book won't teach you how to become a data scientist, but it will give you fairly a decent idea of the ways in which data science is fundamentally altering our world, for better and for worse.

As you might have already guessed, the main audience for this book isn't data scientists, per se. I think it's safe to assume they already love data science, to one degree or another. This book is written primarily for people who want to learn a bit about data science but would rather not sign up for an online class or attend a lecture at their local library.

Careful readers will notice that I rather carelessly use the terms "data science" and "big data" interchangeably, like the way some people use the terms "Middle Ages" and "Medieval Period" interchangeably. I am guilty as charged, and I hope you can forgive me.

Safari® Books Online

 *Safari Books Online* is an on-demand digital library that delivers expert content in both book and video form from the world's leading authors in technology and business.

Technology professionals, software developers, web designers, and business and creative professionals use Safari Books Online as their primary resource for research, problem solving, learning, and certification training.

Safari Books Online offers a range of plans and pricing for enterprise, government, education, and individuals.

Members have access to thousands of books, training videos, and prepublication manuscripts in one fully searchable database from publishers like O'Reilly Media, Prentice Hall Professional, Addison-Wesley Professional, Microsoft Press, Sams, Que, Peachpit Press, Focal Press, Cisco Press, John Wiley & Sons, Syngress, Morgan Kaufmann, IBM Redbooks, Packt, Adobe Press, FT Press, Apress, Manning, New Riders, McGraw-Hill, Jones & Bartlett, Course Technology, and hundreds more. For more information about Safari Books Online, please visit us online.

How to Contact Us

Please address comments and questions concerning this book to the publisher:

O'Reilly Media, Inc.
1005 Gravenstein Highway North
Sebastopol, CA 95472
800-998-9938 (in the United States or Canada)
707-829-0515 (international or local)
707-829-0104 (fax)

We have a web page for this book, where we list errata, examples, and any additional information. You can access this page at *http://bit.ly/learningtolovedatascience*.

To comment or ask technical questions about this book, send email to *bookquestions@oreilly.com*.

For more information about our books, courses, conferences, and news, see our website at *http://www.oreilly.com*.

Find us on Facebook: *facebook.com/oreilly*

Follow us on Twitter: *twitter.com/oreillymedia*

Watch us on YouTube: *www.youtube.com/oreillymedia*

Acknowledgments

This book is a work of journalism, not science. It's based on the aggregated wisdom of many sources, interviewed over the course of several years. All the sources cited in the original reports had the opportunity to review what I'd written about them prior to publication, which I think is a fair practice.

A long time ago, journalists invented an early form of crowdsourcing. We called it "multiple sourcing." Back in the old days, our gruff editors would reflexively spike "one-source" stories. As a result, we learned quickly to include quotes and supporting information from as many sources as possible. Multiple sourcing was also a great CYA (cover your ass) strategy: if you wrote something in a story that turned out to be incorrect, you could always blame the sources.

This book would not have been possible without the cooperation of many expert sources, and I thank them profusely for generously sharing their time and knowledge.

I owe special thanks to Mike Loukides and the wonderfully talented group of editors at O'Reilly Media who worked with me on this project: Holly Bauer, Marie Beaugureau, Susan Conant, and Timothy McGovern. Additionally, I am grateful for the support and guidance provided by Edith Barlow, Greg Fell, Holly Gilthorpe, Cornelia Lévy-Bencheton, Michael Minelli, William Ruh, Joseph Salvo, and Amy Sarociek. Thank you all.

CHAPTER 1

The Culture of Big Data Analytics

Topline Summary

Hollywood loves the myth of a lone scientist working late nights in a dark laboratory on a mysterious island, but the truth is far less melodramatic. Real science is almost always a team sport. Groups of people, collaborating with other groups of people, are the norm in science—and data science is no exception to the rule.

When large groups of people work together for extended periods of time, a culture begins to emerge. This paper, written in the spring of 2013, was an early attempt at describing the people and processes of the emerging culture of data science.

It's Not Just About Numbers

Today's conversational buzz around big data analytics tends to hover around three general themes: technology, techniques, and the imagined future (either bright or dystopian) of a society in which big data plays a significant role in everyday life.

Typically missing from the buzz are in-depth discussions about the people and processes—the cultural bedrock—required to build viable frameworks and infrastructures supporting big data initiatives in ordinary organizations.

Thoughtful questions must be asked and thoroughly considered. Who is responsible for launching and leading big data initiatives? Is it the CFO, the CMO, the CIO, or someone else? Who determines the success or failure of a big data project? Does big data require corporate governance? What does a big data project team look like? Is it a mixed group of people with overlapping skills or a hand-picked squad of highly trained data scientists? What exactly is a data scientist?

Those types of questions skim the surface of the emerging cultural landscape of big data. They remind us that big data—like other so-called technology revolutions of the recent past—is also a cultural phenomenon and has a social dimension. It's vitally important to remember that most people have not considered the immense difference between a world seen through the lens of a traditional relational database system and a world seen through the lens of a Hadoop Distributed File System.

This paper broadly describes the cultural challenges that invariably accompany efforts to create and sustain big data initiatives in a global economy that is increasingly evolving toward the Hadoop perspective, but whose data-management processes and capabilities are still rooted firmly in the traditional architecture of the data warehouse.

The cultural component of big data is neither trivial nor free. It is not a list of "feel-good" or "fluffy" attributes that are posted on a corporate website. Culture (that is, people and processes) is integral and critical to the success of any new technology deployment or implementation. That fact has been demonstrated repeatedly over the past six decades of technology evolution. Here is a brief and incomplete list of recent "technology revolutions" that have radically transformed our social and commercial worlds:

- The shift from vacuum tubes to transistors
- The shift from mainframes to client servers and then to PCs
- The shift from written command lines to clickable icons
- The introduction and rapid adoption of enterprise resource planning (ERP), e-commerce, sales-force automation, and customer relationship management (CRM) systems
- The convergence of cloud, mobile, and social networking systems

Each of those revolutions was followed by a period of intense cultural adjustment as individuals and organizations struggled to capitalize on the many benefits created by the newer technologies. It seems unlikely that big data will follow a different trajectory. Technology does not exist in a vacuum. In the same way that a plant needs water and nourishment to grow, technology needs people and processes to thrive and succeed.

According to Gartner, 4.4 million big data jobs will be created by 2014, and only a third of them will be filled. Gartner's prediction evokes images of "gold rush" for big data talent, with legions of hardcore quants converting their advanced degrees into lucrative employment deals. That scenario promises high times for data analysts in the short term, but it obscures the longer-term challenges facing organizations that hope to benefit from big data strategies.

Hiring data scientists will be the easy part. The real challenge will be integrating that newly acquired talent into existing organizational structures and inventing new structures that will enable data scientists to generate real value for their organizations.

Playing by the Rules

Misha Ghosh is a global solutions leader at MasterCard Advisors, the professional services arm of MasterCard Worldwide. It provides real-time transaction data and proprietary analysis, as well as consulting and marketing services. It's fair to say that MasterCard Advisors is a leader in applied data science. Before joining MasterCard, Ghosh was a senior executive at Bank of America, where he led a variety of data analytics teams and projects. As an experienced practitioner, he knows his way around the obstacles that can slow or undermine big data projects.

"One of the main cultural challenges is securing executive sponsorships," says Ghosh. "You need executive-level partners and champions early on. You also need to make sure that the business folks, the analytics folks, and the technology folks are marching to the same drumbeat."

Instead of trying to stay "under the radar," Ghosh advises big data leaders to play by the rules. "I've seen rogue big data projects pop up, but they tend to fizzle out very quickly," he says. "The old adage that it's better to seek forgiveness afterward than to beg for permission doesn't really hold for big data projects. They are simply too expensive and they require too much collaboration across various parts of the enterprise. So you cannot run them as rogue projects. You need executive buy-in and support."

After making the case to the executive team, you need to keep the spark of enthusiasm alive among all the players involved in supporting or implementing the project. According to Ghosh, "It's critical to maintain the interest and attention of your constituency. After you've laid out a roadmap of the project so everyone knows where they are going, you need to provide them with regular updates. You need to communicate. If you stumble, you need to let them know why you stumbled and what you will do to overcome the barriers you are facing. Remember, there's no clear path for big data projects. It's like *Star Trek*—you're going where no one has gone before."

At present, there is no standard set of best practices for managing big data teams and projects. But an ad hoc set of practices is emerging. "First, you must create transparency," says Ghosh. "Lay out the objectives. State explicitly what you intend to accomplish and which problems you intend to solve. That's absolutely critical. Your big data teams must be 'use case-centric.' In other words, find a problem first and then solve it. That seems intuitive, but I've seen many teams do exactly the opposite: first they create a solution and then they look for a problem to solve."

Marcia Tal pioneered the application of advanced data analytics to real-world business problems. She is best known in the analytics industry for creating and building Citigroup's Decision Management function. Its charter was seeking significant industry breakthroughs for growth across Citigroup's retail and wholesale banking businesses. Starting with three people in 2001, Tal grew the function into a scalable organization with more than 1,000 people working in 30 countries. She left Citi in 2011 and formed her own consulting company, Tal Solutions, LLC.

"Right now, everyone focuses on the technology of big data," says Tal. "But we need to refocus our attention on the people, the processes, the business partnerships, revenue generation, P&L impact, and business results. Most of the conversation has been about generating insights from big data. Instead, we should be talking about how to translate those insights into tangible business results."

Creating a sustainable analytics function within a larger corporate entity requires support from top management, says Tal. But the strength and quality of that support depends on the ability of the analytics function to demonstrate its value to the corporation.

"The organization needs to see a revenue model. It needs to perceive the analytics function as a revenue producer, and not as a cost center. It needs to see the value created by analytics," says Tal. That critical shift in perception occurs as the analytics function forms partnerships with business units across the company and consistently demonstrates the value of its capabilities.

"When we started the Decision Management function at Citi, it was a very small group and we needed to demonstrate our value to the rest of the company. We focused on specific business needs and gaps. We closed the gaps, and we drove revenue and profits. We demonstrated our ability to deliver results. That's how we built our credibility," says Tal.

Targeting specific pain points and helping the business generate more revenue are probably the best strategies for assuring ongoing investment in big data initiatives. "If you aren't focusing on real pain points, you're probably not going to get the commitment you need from the company," says Tal.

No Bucks, No Buck Rogers

Russ Cobb, vice president of marketing and alliances at SAS, also recommends shifting the conversation from technology to people and processes. "The cultural dimension potentially can have a major impact on the success or failure of a big data initiative," says Cobb. "Big data is a hot topic, but technology adoption doesn't equal ROI. A company that doesn't start with at least a general idea of the direction it's heading in and an understanding of how it will define success is not ready for a big data project."

Too much attention is focused on the cost of the investment and too little on the expected return, says Cobb. "Companies try to come up with some measure of ROI, but generally, they put more detail around the 'I' and less detail around the 'R.' It is often easier to calculate costs than it is to understand and articulate the drivers of return."

Cobb sees three major challenges facing organizations with big plans for leveraging big data. The first is not having a clear picture of the destination or desired outcome. The second is hidden costs, mostly in the area of process change. The third and thorniest challenge is organizational. "Are top and middle managers ready to push their decision-making authority out to people on the front lines?" asks Cobb. "One of the reasons for doing big data is that it moves you closer to real-time decision making. But those kinds of decisions tend to be made on the front lines, not in the executive suite. Will management be comfortable with that kind of cultural shift?"

Another way of phrasing the question might be: Is the modern enterprise really ready for big data? Stephen Messer, cofounder and vice chairman of Collective[i], a software-as-a-service business intelligence solution for sales, customer service, and marketing, isn't so sure. "People think this is a technological revolution, but it's really a business revolution enabled by technology," says Messer. Without entrepreneurial leadership from the business, big data is just another technology platform.

"You have to start with the business issue," says Messer. "You need a coalition of people inside the company who share a business problem that can be solved by applying big data. Without that coalition, there is no mission. You have tactics and tools, but you have no strategy. It's not transformational."

Michael Gold, CEO of Farsite, a data analytics firm whose clients include Dick's Sporting Goods and the Ohio State University Medical Center, says it's important to choose projects with manageable scale and clearly defined objectives.

"The questions you answer should be big enough and important enough for people to care," says Gold. "Your projects should create revenue or reduce costs. It's harder to build momentum and maintain enthusiasm for long projects, so keep your projects short. Manage the scope, and make sure you deliver some kind of tangible results."

At a recent Strata + Hadoop World conference in New York, Gold listed three practical steps for broadening support for big data initiatives:

1. Demonstrate ROI for a business use case.
2. Build a team with the skills and ability to execute.
3. Create a detailed plan for operationalizing big data.

"From our perspective, it's very important that all of the data scientists working on a project understand the client's strategic objectives and what problems we're trying to solve for them," says Gold. "Data scientists look at data differently (and better, we think) when they're thinking about answering a business question, not just trying to build the best analytical models."

It's also important to get feedback from clients early and often. "We work in short bursts (similar to a scrum in an Agile methodology) and then present work to clients so they can react to it," says Gold. "That approach ensures that our data scientists incorporate as much of the clients' knowledge into their work as possible. The short cycles require our teams to be focused and collaborative, which is how we've structured our data science groups."

Operationalizing Predictability

The term "data scientist" has been used loosely for several years, leading to a general sense of confusion over the role and its duties. A headline in the October 2012 edition of the *Harvard Business Review*, "Data Scientist: The Sexiest Job of the 21st Century," (*http://bit.ly/hbrdatascience*) had the unintended effect of deepening the mystery.

In 2010, Drew Conway, then a Ph.D. candidate in political science at New York University, created a Venn diagram showing the overlapping skill sets of a data scientist (Figure 1-1). Conway began his career as a computational social scientist in the US intelligence community and has become an expert in applying computational methods to social and behavioral problems at large scale.

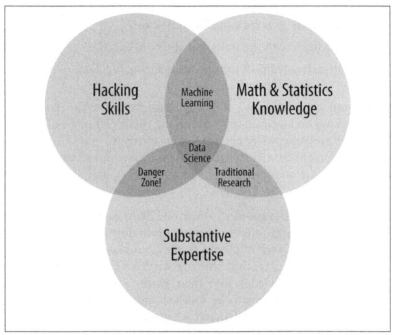

Figure 1-1. Conway's Venn diagram of a data scientist's skill sets

From Conway's perspective, a data scientist should possess the following:

- Hacking skills
- Math and statistical knowledge
- Substantive expertise

All three areas are important, but not everyone is convinced that one individual has to embody all the skills of a data scientist to play a useful role on a big data analytics team.

The key to success, as Michael Gold suggested earlier, is operationalizing the processes of big data. Taking it a step further, it is also important to demystify big data. While the *Harvard Business Review* certainly meant no harm, its headline had the effect of glamorizing rather than clarifying the challenges of big data.

Zubin Dowlaty, vice president of innovation and development at Mu Sigma, a provider of decision science services, envisions a future in which big data has become so thoroughly operationalized and automated that humans are no longer required.

"When I walk into an enterprise today, I see the humans are working at 90 percent capacity and the machines are working at 20 percent capacity," says Dowlaty. "Obviously, the machines are capable of handling more work. Machines, unlike humans, scale up very nicely."

Automation is a necessary step in the development of large-scale systems that feed on big data to generate real-time predictive intelligence. "Anticipation denotes intelligence," says Dowlaty, quoting a line from the science-fiction movie *The Fifth Element*. "Operationalizing predictability is what intelligence is all about."

Assembling the Team

At some point in the future, probably sooner rather than later, Dowlaty's vision of automated big data analytics will no doubt become reality. Until then, however, organizations with hopes of leveraging the potential of big data will have to rely on humans to get the work done.

In a 2012 paper,[1] Sean Kandel, Andreas Paepcke, Joseph Hellerstein, and Jeffrey Heer presented the results of interviews with 35 data analysts working in commercial organizations in healthcare, retail, finance, and social networking. Hellerstein, a professor at UC Berkeley, summarized key findings of the paper at a recent Strata conference. The paper includes insights and models that will likely prove useful to anyone tasked with assembling a big data analytics team. Based on their interviews, the researchers perceive three basic analyst archetypes:

- *Hacker*
- *Scripter*
- *Application user*

The hacker is typically a fluent programmer and manipulator of data. The scripter performs most of his work within an existing soft-

---

1 "Enterprise Data Analysis and Visualization: An Interview Study." (*http://stanford.io/1iwKI36*)

ware package and works mostly on data that has been retrieved from a data warehouse by information technology (IT) staff. The application user relies on spreadsheets or highly specialized applications and typically works on smaller data sets than hackers and scripters.

It is important for management to understand the differences between those types of analysts when staffing a data analytics team. Hackers are more likely to have a background in computer science. "They are folks who have good facility with programming and systems, but less facility with stats and some of the more 'scientific' aspects of data science. They also tend to have less contextual knowledge of the domain-specific questions being explored in the data," explains Hellerstein.

Scripters, on the other hand, are more likely to be trained statisticians, and app users are more likely to be business people. At the risk of oversimplification, a chart showing the three kinds of analysts and their typical academic backgrounds might look something like this:

Analyst type	Training or academic background
Hacker	Computer science major
Scripter	Statistics major
Application user	MBA

"No (single) one of these categories is more likely than another to succeed on its own," says Hellerstein. "You can teach stats and business to a hacker, or you can teach computer science and business to a scripter, or you can teach stats and computer science to an app user."

Scripters and app users would likely require some sort of self-service software to function without help from IT. Similar software might also be useful for hackers, sparing them the drudgery of data prep.

The good news is that several companies are working hard at developing self-service tools that will help analysts become more self-reliant and less dependent on IT. As the tools become more sophisticated and more widely available, it is possible that the distinctions between the three types of analysts might fade or at least become less problematic.

Even when a full suite of practical self-service tools becomes available, it might still make sense to hire a variety of analyst types. For instance, an analytics group that hired only hackers would be like a baseball team that signed only pitchers. Successful teams—whether in business or in sports—tend to include people with various skills, strengths, and viewpoints. Or to put it more bluntly, good luck trying to manage an analytics team made up solely of hackers.

The paper also describes five high-level tasks of data analysis:

- Discovery
- Wrangling
- Profiling
- Modeling
- Reporting

Each of the five tasks has a different workflow, presents a different set of challenges or pain points, and requires a different set of tools. Clearly, the universe of practical analytics is a blend of various tasks, tools, and workflows. More to the point, each stage of the analytics process requires an analyst or analysts with particular skills and a particular mindset.

Not all data analysts are created equal, nor are they likely to share the same zeal for different parts of the process. Some analysts will be better at some aspects of analysis than others. Putting together and managing teams that can handle all the necessary phases of data analysis is a major part of the cultural challenge facing organizations as they ramp up big data initiatives.

Team leadership is another challenge. MasterCard's Ghosh recommends that big data projects "be led by passionate and creative data scientists, not by bureaucrats or finance professionals." Others argue that big data initiatives should be led by seasoned corporate executives with boardroom negotiating skills and a keen understanding of how the C-suite operates.

Some companies have hired a chief analytics officer or created an enterprise analytics group that functions as a shared service, similar to an enterprise IT function. Most companies, however, embed analysts within separate business units.

The advantage of planting analysts in individual business units is that it puts the analysts closer to customers and end users. The downside of spreading analytic expertise among various units includes poor communication, lack of collaboration, and the tendency to reinvent the wheel to solve local problems instead of seeking help from other parts of the enterprise.

Another problem with the decentralized analytics model is lack of governance. Today, it is unusual to find the words "governance" and "analytics" in the same sentence. As big data takes on a higher profile in modern corporations, governance will almost certainly become an issue.

For example, very few data analysts save code or models that do not result in practical solutions to immediate problems. As a consequence, analysts can waste an incredible amount of effort making the same or similar mistakes. Unlike, say, chemistry or biology, in which the results of all experiments are duly noted and logged whether or not they are successful, the precise details of data science experiments are usually captured when the analyst succeeds at solving the particular problem at hand.

Another issue that arises from using Hadoop and other frameworks for handling large amounts of unstructured data is the preservation of documentation and potentially important details about the data.

Sean Kandel, a coauthor of the study referenced earlier, sees the "impulse to dump data into an HDFS" as a growing cultural challenge. "When you have to have a traditional data warehousing environment, there is more of a culture around governance and making sure the data that comes in is well structured and fits the global schema," says Kandel. "When you get away from those established practices, it becomes harder to work with the data."

As Kandel and his coauthors write in their paper:

> With relational databases, organizations typically design a database schema and structure incoming data upon load. This process is often time-consuming and difficult, especially with large complex data sets. With Hadoop, analysts typically take advantage of its ability to operate on less structured data formats. Instead of structuring the data up front during ingest, organizations commonly dump data files into the Hadoop Distributed File System (HDFS)

with little documentation. Analysis of this data then requires parsing the data during Map-Reduce jobs or bulk reformatting to load into relational databases. While remaining unstructured, the data may be difficult to search and profile due to the lack of a defined schema. In some cases, the analysts who originally imported and understood the data may no longer work at the company or may have forgotten important details.

"In a large company," says Kandel, "those people might be hard to find. Now you have some interesting questions: Who is responsible for annotating data? How do you structure the data warehouse? How do you convince people to take the time to label the data properly?"

The lack of a disciplined process—what some would call governance —for handling data at every stage of the analytics process suggests the need for automated systems that capture keystrokes or create audit trails that would make it possible for data scientists to replicate or re-examine the work of other data scientists.

Fitting In

Paul Kent is vice president of big data at SAS, one of the earliest and best-known makers of data analytics. He sees a sort of natural "give and take" between traditional analysts working with limited sets of structured data and a newer generation of analysts who seem comfortable handling an endless deluge of unstructured data.

"I think you have to give the newer analysts their own space. They'll need to preserve some of their independence. They won't be happy playing by the old-school rules," says Kent. "Big data has changed the way we look at data. It's messy, and it's not expensive to save. So we save as much as we can. And when we have questions in the future, we'll map those questions to the data that we've saved."

In the past, data infrastructures were designed around a known set of questions. Today, it's much harder to predict the questions that will be asked. That uncertainty makes it nearly impossible to build traditional-style infrastructures for handling big data.

"We really can't design the perfect structure for data and then just pour data into it," says Kent. "So you have to think about it the other way around. We don't even know the questions we're going to ask tomorrow or next month. So we keep as much data as we can, and we try to be as flexible as possible so we can answer questions when they come up."

The "old-school" perspective was that "if you think real hard, you can design a nice structure for your data and then fill it up whenever you get your data—every week, every day, or every hour," says Kent. If the structure you designed was good enough, it could be tweaked or modified over time to keep up with the changing needs of the market.

"The new school says, 'Nope, that won't work. Let's just save the data as it comes in. We'll merge it and join it and splice it on a case-by-case basis.' The new-school approach doesn't necessarily need a relational database. Sometimes they'll just work with raw files from the originating system," says Kent.

Andreas Weigend teaches at Stanford University and directs the Social Data Lab. The former chief scientist at Amazon, he helped the company build the customer-centric, measurement-focused culture that has become central to its success. Weigend sees data-driven companies following an evolutionary path from "data set to tool set to skill set to mindset." He suggests eight basic rules for organizations in search of a big data strategy:

1. Start with the problem, not with the data.
2. Share data to get data.
3. Align interests of all parties.
4. Make it trivially easy for people to contribute, connect, collaborate.
5. Base the equation of your business on customer-centric metrics.
6. Decompose the business into its "atoms."
7. Let people do what people are good at, and computers what computers are good at.
8. Thou shalt not blame technology for barriers of institutions and society.

Weigend's list of rules focuses entirely on the cultural side of big data. In some ways, it's like the driver's manual you read in high school: heavy on driving etiquette and light on auto mechanics. The miracle of the internal combustion engine is taken for granted. What matters now is traveling safely from point A to point B.

Conversations about big data have moved up the food chain. People seem less interested in the technical details and more interested in how big data can help their companies become more effective, more nimble, and more competitive. As Marcia Tal puts it, "The C-suite wants to know what big data is worth to the organization. They want to see the revenue it generates. They want to understand its value and measure the return on their investment."

CHAPTER 2

Data and Social Good

Topline Summary

Can advances in data science be leveraged for social good? Is there a natural intersection between philanthropy and data science? The early hype around data science emphasized its power to make businesses more profitable and efficient. Is that the only plausible narrative?

Most data scientists are not looking to become software zillionaires. Most of them would prefer to use their skills and knowledge to make the world a better place. This report, written in the winter and spring of 2015, focuses on data scientists and statisticians who improve communities and help humanity in a variety of ways, from preventing teen suicides in American suburbs to raising funds for impoverished farmers in Africa.

Hearts of Gold

Several years ago, large management consulting firms began describing data as the "new oil"—a magically renewable and seemingly inexhaustible source of fuel for spectacular economic growth. The business media rapidly picked up on the idea, and reported breathlessly about the potential for data to generate untold riches for those wise enough to harness its awesome power.

At the same time, another story was unfolding. That story wasn't about a few smart guys getting rich. It was about people using data to improve lives and make the world a better place.

For many of us, it's an alluring narrative, perhaps because it supports our hope that deep down, data scientists and statisticians are nice people who value social good over crass materialism.

Megan Price, for example, is director of research at the Human Rights Data Analysis Group (*https://hrdag.org*). She designs strategies and methods for using data to support human rights projects in strife-torn countries like Guatemala, Colombia, and Syria. "I've always been interested in both statistics and social justice," Price says. In college, she started off as a math major, switched to statistics, and later studied public health in grad school. "I was surrounded by people who were all really invested in using their math and science skills for social justice. It was a great environment for bringing those interests together."

In Guatemala, Price serves as lead statistician on a project in which she analyzes documents from the National Police Archive. She helped her colleagues prepare evidence for high-profile court cases involving Guatemalan officials implicated in kidnappings. By rigorously analyzing data from government records, Price and her colleagues revealed clear links between the officials and the crimes. In Syria, she was lead statistician and author on three reports commissioned by the United Nations Office of the High Commissioner for Human Rights (OHCHR) (*http://bit.ly/1WiFxCQ*).

"I'd like to think that many statisticians and data scientists would do that kind of work if they had the chance," she says. "But it can be difficult to find the right opportunities. Doing pro bono work is a lovely idea, but there are limits to what you can accomplish by volunteering a few hours on nights and weekends. Many projects require full-time commitment."

Price hopes to see an increase in "formal opportunities" for data scientists to work on noncommercial, socially relevant projects. "Right now, there are very few organizations hiring full-time data scientists for social justice. I'm hoping that will change over the next 10 to 15 years."

Structuring Opportunities for Philanthropy

In many ways, DataKind (*http://www.datakind.org/*) is a harbinger of the future that Price envisions. DataKind is nonprofit that connects socially minded data scientists with organizations working to address critical humanitarian issues. "We're dedicated to tackling the world's greatest problems with data science," says Jake Porway, DataKind's founder and executive director. "We connect people whose day jobs are on Wall Street or in Silicon Valley with mission-driven organizations that can use data to make a positive impact on the world."

DataKind's programs range from short-term engagements done over a weekend to long-term, multimonth projects. All programs bring together data scientists and social-change organizations to collaborate on meaningful projects that move the needle on humanitarian challenges.

For example, when data scientists at Teradata (*http://bit.ly/1ORV0ra*) were looking for new and improved ways to apply their skills to philanthropy, they teamed up with DataKind. The two organizations co-hosted a weekend "DataDive" that provided an opportunity for data scientists from DataKind and Teradata to work collaboratively with nonprofits and humanitarian organizations such as iCouldBe (*http://www.icouldbe.org/*), HURIDOCS (*https://www.huridocs.org/*), GlobalGiving (*http://www.globalgiving.org/*), and the Cultural Data Project (*http://www.culturaldata.org/*) on a wide range of data challenges, from improving an online mentoring program for at-risk youth to tracking human rights cases in Europe.

"One thing we found is there is no lack of demand for these services. We have over 200 organizations that have submitted applications to receive some sort of data science services," Porway says. "On the other side, we should mention, we have more than 5,000 people who have signed up to volunteer. There is demand on both sides."

In many instances, the challenge is combining or integrating data from disparate sources. In London, DataKind UK, one of the organization's six chapters worldwide, helped St Mungo's Broadway (*http://www.mungosbroadway.org.uk/*), a charity that helps people deal with issues leading to homelessness, link its data with data from Citizens Advice (*http://www.citizensadvice.org.uk/*), a national charity providing free information on civil matters to the public. Linking the data yielded a trove of new insights that made it easier for St Mungo's Broadway to predict which clients were more likely to benefit from its support.

In India, DataKind works with Simpa Networks (*http://simpanet works.com/*), a venture-backed technology company in India that sells solar-as-a-service to energy-poor households and small businesses. Simpa's mission is making sustainable energy "radically affordable" to the 1.6 billion people at the "base of the pyramid" who currently lack access to affordable electricity.

In a six-month project financially underwritten by MasterCard, a team of DataKind volunteers is using Simpa Networks' historical data on customer payment behavior to predict which new applicants are likely to be a good fit for its model. That will enable Simpa Networks to best serve its customers and better assess new customers to offer the most appropriate services and support.

"Our goal is offering energy services to everyone, which includes customers who otherwise would be 'unbankable' according to mainstream financial institutions," says Paul Needham, Simpa Networks' chairman and CEO.

Data analytics plays a major role in supporting Simpa's ambitious mission. "Customer usage and payment behaviors are constantly tracked, and the data is fed into our proprietary credit-scoring model. That helps us get smarter about selecting customers and allows us to take risks on rural farmers that some banks would be uncomfortable financing," Needham says.

The energy situation is especially dire in India, where 75 million families have no access to electricity, and enormous sums are spent on unclean fuels such as kerosene for lanterns. "The good news is that effective decentralized energy solutions already exist. Solar photovoltaic solutions such as solar home systems can be sized appropriately to meet the energy needs of rural households and small businesses," Needham says. With data analytics, Simpa can make the case for loaning money that can be applied to clean-energy systems.

"Having learned from our past impact evaluation results, we have sufficient evidence to support the fact that Simpa's clean energy service will significantly reduce the time needed to conduct farming work, household chores, cooking, and cleaning," Needham says.

"We anticipate that overall health standards will improve in these households due to the improved quality of light and will encourage the move away from kerosene and other hazardous forms of energy usage. In our midline impact evaluation study, we have seen that 80 percent of customers surveyed suffered eye irritation due to smoke; after Simpa's intervention, this figure dropped to 28 percent. Similarly, 10 percent of customers surveyed experienced fire accidents; after Simpa's intervention, this figure dropped to zero. We also believe that shop owners in these energy-poor areas will be able to stay open longer hours, which is likely to increase their sales and overall productivity."

Telling the Story with Analytics

DataKind also has collaborated with Crisis Text Line (*http://www.crisistextline.org/*) (CTL), a free service providing emotional support and information for anyone in a crisis. The process for accessing help is simple and efficient: people in need of help send texts to CTL, and trained specialists respond to the texts with support, counseling, information, and referrals.

CTL is staffed by volunteers, and like all volunteer organizations, its resources are constrained. CTL's mission is providing potentially life-saving support services for people in need—but it's also critical for the organization to avoid overwhelming its volunteers.

"Repeat callers have posed a challenge for crisis centers since the 1970s," explains Bob Filbin, CTL's chief data scientist. "When you read through the academic literature, you see that repeat callers are a big difficulty for crisis centers."

It's not that CTL's counselors don't want to help everyone who texts them—it's just that some people who contact CTL need a rapid intervention to avert a tragedy. The hard part is figuring out which people are experiencing acute, short-term crises requiring immediate attention and which people are suffering from less acute problems that can be dealt with over a slightly longer time frame.

After analyzing data from thousands of texts and examining patterns of usage from academic literature, Filbin and his colleagues were able to make suggestions for managing the problem of repeat texters. "We realized that our counselors were spending 34 percent of their time with 3 percent of our texters. By rolling out new policies and new technical products, we were able to reduce the portion of time our counselors spent with repeat texters from 34 percent to 8 percent. It was a huge win for us because it allowed more people to use the service."

In addition to freeing up more time for volunteers to interact with people experiencing acute problems, CTL was able to improve service for the repeat texters by guiding them toward helpful long-term resources.

Using data analysis to boost CTL's ability to deliver potentially life-saving services to people in need is especially gratifying, Filbin says. "It's very exciting when we can use data to overturn existing assumptions or drive meaningful change through an organization. Bringing data to bear on the problem, measuring our progress, and evaluating the effectiveness of our policies and products—it all makes an enormous difference."

From Filbin's perspective, it all comes down to good storytelling. "Data is only valuable when people act on it. Framing the data in terms of saving time was an emotional trigger that helped people understand its value," he says. "By reducing the conversation minutes with repeat texters from 34 percent down to 8 percent, we suddenly saved a quarter of our volunteers' time. That's a powerful story."

The idea of using data as a tool for storytelling is a recurring theme among data scientists working in philanthropic organizations. Most of the data scientists interviewed for this report mentioned storytelling as an important output of their work. Essentially, a good story makes it easier for managers and executives to make decisions and to take action on the insights generated by the data science team.

Data as a Pillar of Modern Democracy

Emma Mulqueeny, who writes a popular blog on data science, sees a larger trend evolving. Mulqueeny is the founder of Rewired State (*http://www.rewiredstate.org/*) and Young Rewired State (*http://www.yrs.io/*), a commissioner for the Speaker's Commission on Digital Democracy (*http://bit.ly/1KA03Gs*) in the UK, a Google Fellow, and a digital tech entrepreneur. Earlier in her career, while working for the UK government on digital communication strategies, she noticed a sea change in the way people responded to statements made by government officials.

"There was a huge scandal over expenses," she recalls, "and suddenly it seemed as though everybody lost their trust in everything the government was saying. Suddenly, everybody wanted facts. They didn't want your interpretation of facts; they just wanted facts."

Government officials were aghast. But as a result of the scandal, efforts were made to increase transparency. Data that previously had been off-limits or difficult to obtain was made available to the public. Data.Gov.UK (*http://data.gov.uk/*) and Data.Gov (*http://www.data.gov/*), both launched in 2009, are prime examples of the "open data" trend in democratic societies. It's almost as if governments are saying, "You want data? We got your data right here!"

Mulqueeny sees those kinds of efforts as steps in the right direction, but she's adamant about the need for doing more. "The way people are operating online, the way they're learning, sharing, and influencing is very much dependent on what's pushed into their space," she says. "We're all familiar with Google's machine learning algorithms. You search for 'blue trousers' and suddenly everywhere you go after that, you're seeing little adverts for blue trousers and other items to buy. Marketers know how to mark up data so it can be used for marketing."

Democratically elected governments, on the other hand, are still struggling with data. "Let's say you feel passionate about chickens. If the information is properly marked up, you are more likely to see when the government is discussing matters related to chickens," Mulqueeny says. "Now let's say the government decides to outlaw chickens in London. If the information is marked up, you'll probably see it. But if it's not properly marked up, you won't. Which means that you won't find out the government is considering banning chickens until you read about it in a newspaper or some other media outlet."

From Mulqeeny's perspective, real democracy requires more than just sharing data—it requires making sure that data is properly tagged, annotated, and presented to people when they are online. In effect, she is raising the bar for governments and saying they need to be as good as—or better than—online marketers when it comes to serving up information.

"People have expectations that their interests will be served in the space in which they choose to be online and that they will find out what's happening when they are online," she says. "That's the heart of everything at the moment."

No Strings Attached, but Plenty of Data

For as long as most of us can remember, charities have worked like this: people or organizations make donations to charities, and charities distribute the donations to people or organizations that need support. Recently, and for a variety of legitimate reasons, the validity of that model has been called into question. As a result, new models for charitable giving have emerged.

GiveDirectly (*https://www.givedirectly.org/*) is an organization that channels donations directly to the extreme poor in Kenya and Uganda. The money is distributed via mobile phones, which makes it relatively easy to keep precise digital records of who's getting what from whom. GiveDirectly's model was inspired by programs initiated by the Mexican government in the 1990s. Those programs showed that direct cash transfers to poor people were often more helpful than benefits that were distributed indirectly.

The "secret formula" behind GiveDirectly's success is scientific discipline. Two of the group's cofounders, Michael Faye and Paul Niehaus, describe the differences between GiveDirectly and traditional charities:

> From the very beginning, we took a principled stand and decided to run randomized trials, which are the gold standard for discovering whether something works or doesn't. Some people can always find excuses for not running randomized trials. They will say they're too expensive or they take too much time or they might jeopardize the business model.
>
> Our response to those excuses is to ask, 'Would you buy drugs from a pharmaceutical company that doesn't run randomized trials of its drugs?' Of course you wouldn't. So why would you donate money to a charity that doesn't test its programs?

Although GiveDirectly distributes donations with no strings attached, its approach is the antithesis of just throwing money at problems. True to their roots as trained economists, Faye and Niehaus have devised an excruciatingly detailed system for making sure donations are used properly. After choosing a village or area to receive donations, GiveDirectly sends a team to the location. The team goes from house to house, creating a highly detailed, data-rich map of the location. Then a second team is dispatched to register local inhabitants and verify the data assembled by the first team.

No money is distributed until a third team has verified the information provided by the first two teams, and even then, only token payments are made to make absolutely sure the money winds up in the right hands. When all the tests are complete, additional payments are authorized, flowing directly to the local residents via mobile banking or other forms of digital cash transfer.

It's a rigorous approach, but it's an approach that can be scaled and audited easily. Transparency, redundancy, and continual analysis are crucial to the success of the overall process. "We think it's the future of charity in the developing world. In fact, we don't see ourselves as a charity—we see ourselves as service providers," Faye says.

GiveDirectly draws a distinction between data and evidence. "We emphasize that understanding impact requires not just knowing what happened, but what knowing *would* have happened if we hadn't intervened," Faye says. "We do that with randomized controlled trials."

Faye and Niehaus urge donors to ask basic questions of all charitable organizations:

- Where exactly does a donated dollar go? Who are the beneficiaries and how much money ultimately winds up in their hands?
- Beyond data alone, do the organizations have evidence showing the impact of their interventions?
- Are the organizations doing more good per dollar than the poor could do by themselves?

Collaboration Is Fundamental

When the New York City Department of Health and Mental Hygiene (*http://bit.ly/nycdohmh*) (DOHMH) realized that restaurant reviews posted on Yelp (*http://www.yelp.com/*) could be a source of valuable information in the ongoing battle to prevent foodborne illnesses, the department reached out to Yelp and to data scientists at Columbia University for help.

Over a nine-month period, roughly 294,000 Yelp reviews were screened by software that had been "trained" to look for potential cases of foodborne disease. According to an article (*http://1.usa.gov/1QZQ2YA*) posted on the Centers for Disease Control and Prevention (*http://www.cdc.gov/*) (CDC) website, "the software flagged 893 reviews for evaluation by an epidemiologist, resulting in the identification of 468 reviews that were consistent with recent or potentially recent foodborne illness."

The article notes that only 3 percent of flagged reviews described events that had been reported to the health department. While the absolute numbers involved were relatively small, the project represents a major victory for data science.

Expending all of that effort to identify a handful of potentially dangerous restaurants in New York City might not seem like a big deal, but imagine scaling the process and offering it to every health department in the world.

"Data is everywhere now, more so than ever before in history," says Luis Gravano, a professor of computer science at Columbia University who worked with the health department on the Yelp project. "Regular people now are leaving a rich trail of incredibly valuable information, through the content they post online and via their mobile devices." Increasingly, data that people generate over the course of their daily lives is picked up by sensors. That kind of passively generated data is "less explicit, but also potentially quite valuable," Gravano says.

The data generated by "regular people" represents a unique opportunity for data scientists. "Collectively, the data is a great resource for all of us who analyze data," he says. "But the challenge is finding the gold nuggets of information in these mountains of data."

Dr. Sharon Balter, an epidemiologist at the health department, says data science was the key to finding the important pieces of information hidden in the reviews. "The team from Columbia helped us focus on the small number of restaurant reviews that might indicate real problems. The challenge is sifting through thousands of reviews. We don't have the resources to investigate every one of them," Balter says. "The algorithms developed by the Columbia team helped us determine which leads to investigate, and that was incredibly helpful."

Here's how the process worked, according to the CDC article:

Beginning in April 2012, Yelp provided DOHMH with a private data feed of New York City restaurant reviews. The feed provided data publicly available on the website but in an XML format, and text classification programs were trained to automatically analyze reviews. For this pilot project, a narrow set of criteria were chosen to identify those reviews with a high likelihood of describing foodborne illness. Reviews were assessed retrospectively, using the following criteria: 1) presence of the keywords "sick," "vomit," "diarrhea," or "food poisoning" in contexts denoting foodborne illness; 2) two or more persons reported ill; and 3) an incubation period ≥10 hours.

Ten hours was chosen because most foodborne illnesses are not caused by toxins but rather by organisms with an incubation period of ≥10 hours (1). Data mining software was used to train the text classification programs (2). A foodborne disease epidemiologist manually examined output results to determine whether reviews selected by text classification met the criteria for inclusion, and programs with the highest accuracy rate were incorporated into the final software used for the pilot project to analyze reviews prospectively.

The software program downloaded weekly data and provided the date of the restaurant review, a link to the review, the full review text, establishment name, establishment address, and scores for each of three outbreak criteria (i.e., keywords, number of persons ill, and incubation period), plus an average of the three criteria. Scores for individual criteria ranged from 0 to 1, with a score closer to 1 indicating the review likely met the score criteria.

Reviews submitted to Yelp during July 1, 2012–March 31, 2013 were analyzed. All reviews with an average review score of ≥0.5 were evaluated by a foodborne disease epidemiologist. Because the average review score was calculated by averaging the individual criteria scores, reviews could receive an average score of ≥0.5 without meeting all individual criteria.

Reviews with an average review score of ≥0.5 were evaluated for the following three criteria: 1) consistent with foodborne illness occurring after a meal, rather than an alternative explanation for the illness keyword; 2) meal date within 4 weeks of review (or no meal date provided); 3) two or more persons ill or a single person with symptoms of scombroid poisoning or severe neurologic illness. Reviews that met all three of these criteria were then investigated further by DOHMH. In addition, reviews were investigated further if manual checking identified multiple reviews within 1 week that described recent foodborne illness at the same restaurant.

Gravano and Balter agree that the availability of "nontraditional" data was critical to the success of their endeavor. "We're no longer relying solely on traditional sources of data to generate useful insights," Gravano says. As a result, groups of people that were previously "uncounted" can now benefit from the work of data scientists. "We're setting up an infrastructure that will make those kinds of projects more routine. Our hope, moving forward, is that our work will become a continuous process and that we will continually refine our algorithms and machine learning tools," he says.

Recently, another group of researchers at Columbia used machine learning tools to better understand and predict preterm births, a healthcare issue affecting 12–13 percent of infants born in the US. That study relied on a clinical-trial data set collected by the National Institute of Child Health and Human Development (*http://1.usa.gov/1LO2wy9*) (NICHD) and the Maternal-Fetal Medicine Units Network (*http://1.usa.gov/1KBf5g6*) (MFMU).

Conclusion

Most of the sources interviewed for this report highlighted the multidisciplinary and inherently collaborative nature of data science, and several expressed the belief that at some level, most data scientists see their roles as beneficial to society. That said, there still appears to be a clear need for organizations that provide structures and processes for enabling the collaboration and teamwork necessary for effective pro bono data science projects. In other words, doing data science for the good of humankind requires more than good intentions—it requires practical frameworks, networks of qualified people, and sources of funding.

Applying data science principles to solve social problems and improve the lives of ordinary people seems like a logical idea, but it is by no means a given. Using data science to elevate the human condition won't happen by accident; groups of people will have to envision it, develop the routine processes and underlying infrastructures required to make it practical, and then commit the time and energy necessary to make it all work.

Columbia University has taken a step in the right direction by launching the Data Science Institute (*http://datascience.columbia.edu/*), an interdisciplinary learning and research facility with dedicated faculty and six specialized centers: Cybersecurity (*http://*

datascience.columbia.edu/cybersecurity), Financial and Business Analytics (*http://datascience.columbia.edu/financial-and-business-analytics*), Foundations of Data Science (*http://datascience.colum bia.edu/foundations-of-data-science*), Health Analytics (*http:// datascience.columbia.edu/health-analytics*), New Media (*http://data science.columbia.edu/new-media*), and Smart Cities (*http://data science.columbia.edu/smart-cities*).

"Whatever good you want to do in the world, the data is there to make it possible," says Kathleen McKeown, director of the Data Science Institute. "Whether it's finding new and unexpected treatments for disease or techniques for predicting the impact of natural disasters, data science has tremendous potential to benefit society."

Author's Note

Crisis Text Line is looking for volunteers. If you are interested in becoming a crisis counselor, please visit www.crisistextline.org/join-our-efforts/volunteer/ for more information.

DataKind is also seeking volunteers. If you're a data scientist looking to use your skills to give back, you can apply to volunteer with Data-Kind at www.datakind.org/getinvolved/ or learn more at an upcoming event in your area: http://www.datakind.org/community-events/.

CHAPTER 3

Will Big Data Make IT Infrastructure Sexy Again?

Topline Summary

Despite healthy levels of skepticism over the "staying power" of big data (people never tired of asking me when big data would jump the shark and sink ingloriously into the pit of forgotten trends), the impact of big data has been inescapable across the information technology industry. Big data not only hasn't died; it's grown bigger and messier.

As a result, there's been a surge in spending on new and improved infrastructure required for moving massive amounts of data from point A to point B at the fastest possible speed. There's also been a push for newer kinds of computing systems that can collect, store, analyze, and present information at nearly real-time velocities.

This paper, written in the winter of 2014, countered then-popular notions that big data would have minimal impact on IT spending and that the big data trend itself would burn out quickly.

Moore's Law Meets Supply and Demand

Love it or hate it, big data seems to be driving a renaissance in IT infrastructure spending. IDC, for example, estimates that worldwide spending for infrastructure hardware alone (servers, storage, PCs, tablets, and peripherals) will rise from $461 billion in 2013 to $468 billion in 2014. Gartner predicts that total IT spending will grow 3.1 percent in 2014, reaching $3.8 trillion, and forecasts "consistent 4 to 5 percent annual growth through 2017." For a lot of people, the mere thought of all that additional cash makes IT infrastructure seem sexy again.

Big data impacts IT spending directly and indirectly. The direct effects are less dramatic, largely because adding terabytes to a Hadoop cluster is much less costly than adding terabytes to an enterprise data warehouse (EDW). That said, IDG Enterprise's 2014 Big Data survey indicates that more than half of the IT leaders polled believe "they will have to re-architect the data center network to some extent" to accommodate big data services.

The indirect effects are more dramatic, thanks in part to Rubin's law (derived by Dr. Howard Rubin, the unofficial dean of IT economics), which holds that demand for technology rises as the cost of technology drops (which it invariably will, according to Moore's law). Since big data essentially "liberates" data that had been "trapped" in mainframes and EDWs, the demand for big data services will increase as organizations perceive the untapped value at their fingertips. In other words, as utilization of big data goes up, spending on big data services and related infrastructure will also rise. "Big data has the same sort of disruptive potential as the client-server revolution of 30 years ago, which changed the whole way that IT infrastructure evolved," says Marshall Presser, field chief technology officer at Pivotal, a provider of application and data infrastructure software. "For some people, the disruption will be exciting, and for others, it will be threatening."

For IT vendors offering products and services related to big data, the future looks particularly rosy. IDC predicts stagnant (0.7 percent) growth of legacy IT products and high-volume (15 percent) growth of cloud, mobile, social, and big data products—the so-called "Third Platform" of IT. According to IDC, "Third Platform technologies and solutions will drive 29 percent of 2014 IT spending and 89 percent of all IT spending growth." Much of that growth will come from the "cannibalization" of traditional IT markets.

Viewed from that harrowing perspective, maybe "scary" is a better word than "sexy" to describe the looming transformation of IT infrastructure.

Change Is Difficult

As Jennifer Lawrence's character in *American Hustle* notes, change is hard. Whenever something new arrives, plenty of people just cannot resist saying, "It's no big deal, nothing really different, same old stuff in a new package," or words to that effect. And to some extent, they're usually right—at least initially.

Consider the shift from propellers to jet engines. A jet plane looks similar to a propeller-driven plane—it has wings, a fuselage, a tail section, and the same basic control surfaces. But the introduction of jet engines completely transformed the passenger aviation industry by allowing planes to fly higher, faster, longer, and more cost-effectively than ever before. The reason we don't think twice about stepping into airliners is largely because of jet engines, which are significantly more reliable—and much quieter—than propellers.

Two or three years ago, when you asked a CIO about data, the standard reply was something like, "Don't worry, we're capturing all the data we create and saving it."

Here are the sobering realities: no databases are big enough and no networks are fast enough to handle the enormous amounts of data generated by the combination of growing information technologies such as cloud, mobile, social, and the infelicitously named "Internet of Things." A new push by large companies toward "zero unplanned downtime," a strategy that depends on steady flows of data from advanced sensors, will undoubtedly contribute to the glut.

If we conceptualize the relationship between data and insight over the past three decades, it looks something like the following figure:

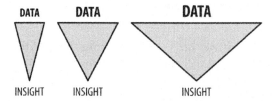

Obviously, the funnels are not drawn to scale, but you get the idea. The mouth of the funnel keeps getting wider to accommodate greater amounts of data, while the spout of the funnel at the bottom remains narrow. At what point does it stop making sense to keep throwing data into the top of the funnel?

Let's say that for a variety of reasons (mostly legal and regulatory), we decide to keep collecting as much data as we possibly can. How are we going to manage all of that new data, and where will we put it? The answer is deceptively simple: not all of that new data will be sent back to a data warehouse and saved; most of it will be evaluated and analyzed closer to its point of origin. Throw away the funnel model—more decisions will be made at the edges of systems, by smart devices and increasingly by smart sensors, which are all part of the new and expanding universe of IT infrastructure.

Fred Thiel is an IT industry expert, serial entrepreneur, and adviser to private equity and venture capital firms. He offers this scenario illustrating how the intersection of big data and the Internet of Things will lead to substantial changes in IT infrastructure:

> You have a pump operating somewhere. The pump is equipped with a sensor that's connected to a data gateway at the edge of a data network. And you know that, compared to ambient temperature, the operating temperature of the pump should be X, ±10 percent. As long as the pump operates within its parametric norm, the system that listens to it and monitors its performance isn't going to report any data. But the minute the pump's temperature or performance breaks through one of its parametric norms, the system will report the event and give you a log of its data for the past 30 seconds, or whatever time interval is appropriate for the system.

Now imagine that scenario playing out all over the world, all the time, in every situation in which data is being generated. Instead of infrastructure that's engineered to capture data and send it back to a data center, you need infrastructure engineered to capture data and make choices in real time, based on the context and value of the data itself.

That kind of infrastructure is a far cry from the traditional IT infrastructure that was basically designed to help the CFO close the company's book faster than the manual accounting systems that preceded IT. It's easy to forget that, for many years, IT's primary purpose was to automate the company's accounting processes. A surprising number of those original systems are still kicking around, adding to the pile of "legacy spaghetti" that CIOs love to complain about.

What we're witnessing now, however, is a somewhat bumpy transition from the old kind of IT that faced mostly inward, to a new kind of IT that faces mostly outward. The old IT dealt mostly with historical information, whereas the new IT is expected to deal with the realities of the outside world, which happens to be the world in which the company's customers and business partners live. Another way of saying this is that after years of resistance, IT is following the nearly universal business trend of replacing product-centricity with customer-centricity.

An extreme example of this trend is bespoke manufacturing, in which Henry Ford's concept of an assembly line turning out millions of the exact same product is stood on its head. In bespoke manufacturing, product development isn't locked into a cycle with a beginning, middle, and end. Product development is iterative and continuous. Cutting-edge processes such as 3D printing and additive manufacturing make it possible to refine and improve products *ad infinitum*, based on user feedback and data sent back to the manufacturing floor by sensors embedded in the products.

Jordan Husney is strategy director for Undercurrent, a digital strategy firm and think tank. His interests include "extending the digital nervous system to distant physical objects," and he provides advisory services for several Fortune 100 companies. From his perspective, the challenge is rapidly scaling systems to meet unexpected levels of demand. "I call it the 'curse of success' because if the market suddenly loves your product, you have to scale up very quickly. Those kinds of scaling problems are difficult to solve, and there isn't a universal toolkit for achieving scalability on the Internet of Things," he says. "When Henry Ford needed to scale up production, he could add another assembly line."

In modern manufacturing scenarios, however, finished products are often assembled from parts that are designed and created in multiple locations, all over the world. When that's the case, it's more important to standardize the manufacturing processes than it is to standardize the parts. "The new edge for standards isn't the part itself; it's the process that makes the part," says Husney. "That type of approach, as manufacturing becomes increasingly bespoke, is going to ripple backward through the organization. The organization is going to have to be on its toes to handle that new kind of standard, in which the process is the standard, not the final product."

The future of fabrication will involve increasingly seamless integrations of digital and mechanical technologies. "Imagine a team that's designing a new part for a complex machine, and while they're designing the part, every time their design application automatically saves a file, the file is sent into the cloud and evaluated by an application that automatically calculates the cost of producing the part, the time required to produce it, and the feasibility of producing it," says Husney. Any segment of the design that is judged infeasible or uneconomical will be highlighted, in real time, by the team's design application. "If we look at that scenario from an IT perspective, we really have to consider whether we have the IT infrastructure necessary to make that future possible."

The new modes of iterative manufacturing and bespoke fabrication will require IT infrastructure that connects and orchestrates interactions between smarter devices, smarter networks, and smarter sensors. The table stakes, it would seem, have gone up.

Meanwhile, Back at the Ranch…

Mike Olson is the founder and chief strategy officer of Cloudera, an early champion of Hadoop for enterprise users and a leading provider of analytic data management services. In many ways, Olson's story is similar to the stories of other highly successful tech entrepreneurs. But it tracks nicely with the emerging narrative of how big data is transforming IT infrastructure. At Berkeley, Olson studied under the legendary Michael Stonebraker, whose research was critical to the development of modern relational database systems. After leaving Berkeley, Olson spent the next couple of decades building database products. He helped launch a series of successful tech firms and made good money in the process. "We built great products, but it wasn't like you woke up with your heart pounding. Over those decades, relational databases just became the default answer to any kind of data management problem," says Olson.

While Olson was building relational databases for big companies, Google was dealing with its own unique data challenge. Google's mission was to vacuum up all the available data on the Web, index it, and make it searchable. Accomplishing that mission required a new approach to data management, something that went far beyond the abilities of relational database technology. Google's solutions were Google File System (GFS) and MapReduce, which was essential to the subsequent development of Hadoop. "In 2004, Google published a couple of papers about GFS and MapReduce, and most of us in the relational database industry thought it was a joke. We totally disregarded it," Olson recalls. "It didn't use SQL, which we *knew* was crucial to data management. What we didn't know was that Google wasn't trying to build a database system that solved the same problems as ours did. Google was building a system that addressed a new problem, at a new scale, and handled complex data from many different sources."

Four years later, Olson and some of his friends revisited Google's research and saw the potential for creating a new industry based on Hadoop. Their driving force was big data—back in 2004, only Google and a handful of other companies were focused on solving big data problems. By 2008, big data had become more widely understood as a serious challenge (or opportunity, depending on your perspective) for organizations worldwide. Machine-to-machine interactions were creating huge volumes of new data, and at astonishing speeds. Suddenly, database managers and database providers were in the hot seat.

Olson describes the transition: "In the old days, when you wanted to build a data center, you called Sun Microsystems and you ordered the biggest box they had. They'd ship it to you as a single centralized server. Then you'd take whatever money you had left over and send it to Oracle, and they'd sell you a license to run their database software on the box. That's where you put all of your data. But machine-generated data grows faster than any box can handle. A single, centralized system can't scale rapidly enough to keep up with all the new data."

Google perceived that an entirely new approach to database management was necessary. "They took what were essentially a bunch of cheap pizza boxes and created a massively parallel infrastructure for managing data at scale. That was Google's genius, and it's changed the way we build data centers, forcing us to design new data management architectures for large enterprises."

Throwing Out the Baby with the Bathwater?

There is a difference of opinion over the extent to which newer data management systems based on open source Hadoop will replace or augment traditional systems such as those offered by Microsoft, IBM, and Oracle.

Abhishek Mehta is founder and CEO of Tresata, a company that builds analytic software for Hadoop environments. From his perspective, HDFS is the future of data management technology. "HDFS is a complete replacement for not just one, but four different layers of the traditional IT stack," says Mehta. "The HDFS ecosystem does storage, processing, analytics, and BI/visualization, all without moving the data back and forth from one system to another. It's a complete cannibalization of the existing stack."

He predicts that companies without HDFS capabilities will find themselves lagging Hadoop-equipped competitors. "The game is over, and HDFS has won the battle," says Mehta. "The biggest problem we see is companies that haven't made HDFS a core part of their IT infrastructure. Not enough companies have HDFS in production environments. But here's the good news: they have no choice. The economics of the traditional systems no longer make sense. Why pay $10,000 per terabyte to store data when you can pay much less? There's a reason why dinosaurs are extinct."

Jorge A. Lopez is director of product marketing at Syncsort, a software firm specializing in data integration. Founded in 1968 by graduates of New York University and Columbia University, Syncsort develops products and services for Hadoop, Windows, UNIX, Linux, and mainframe systems. "We don't recommend throwing out the baby with the bathwater," says Lopez. "Organizations have spent the past decade building up their architectures. But increasing volumes of data create new tensions, and as a result, organizations are weighing trade-offs."

In business there is an old saying: "You can have it fast; you can have it good; you can have it cheap. Pick two." As the volume, velocity, and variety of big data continue to climb, something's gotta give. "If your costs are growing at the same pace as your data, that's a huge problem. If your costs are growing faster than your data, it becomes economically impossible to keep up," says Lopez. Hadoop gives companies a wider range of choices when making trade-offs. "You can shift workloads from your mainframe to Hadoop, which reduces or defers your costs and also lets you start building the skills within your IT organization that will be essential in the future," says

Lopez. "You save a ton of money, and you address the skills gap, which is becoming a really serious issue for many companies."

In the scenario described by Lopez, ETL (extract, transform, load) is the low-hanging fruit. The money you save by shifting ETL workloads from traditional systems into HDFS could be invested in research, product development, or new infrastructure. "Don't get me wrong, I'm not saying that now you can get rid of your Teradata implementation. But ETL uses a large percentage of your Teradata resources and it doesn't add value. If you shift that workload to Hadoop, you have free capacity in your Teradata box and you can do work that adds real value," says Lopez. "To me, a sign that Hadoop is maturing is that big companies in retail, finance, and telecommunications are looking at Hadoop as a way of saving mainframe costs and leveraging data that was previously unusable. Believe it or not, lots of those companies still use tape to store data, and once it's been formatted for tape, the data becomes very difficult to access."

For people of a certain generation, tape drives were sexy—along with hula hoops, marble ashtrays, and Brigitte Bardot.

"It's not that the old architecture wasn't sexy; it's that the new architecture creates very tangible value in terms of being able to draw insights from data in a variety of ways," says Jim Walker, director of product marketing at Hortonworks, an early leader in the Hadoop movement. "We're re-architecting the data center so we can interact with it in multiple different ways simultaneously. It's the whole concept of schema-on-read as opposed to schema-on-write that's transforming the way we think about queries and the way we provide value to the enterprise with data."

For big data evangelists, what's sexy about new IT infrastructure is its potential for delivering insights that lead to better—and more profitable—business decisions. Delivering those kinds of value-added insights requires IT systems that allow users to ask a much more varied set of questions than they can today. "We're maturing toward a contextual-query model. We're definitely still far away from it, but we're setting the IT infrastructure in place that will make it possible," says Walker. "That's what it's really all about."

API-ifiying the Enterprise

Greater accessibility of data at significantly lower costs sounds like a solid argument in favor of modernizing your IT infrastructure. But wait—there's more. As Jorge Lopez suggested earlier, big data technologies also create opportunities for learning new skills and transforming the culture of IT.

Rick Bullotta is cofounder and CTO at ThingWorx, an application platform for the Internet of Things. From his perspective, big data isn't merely transforming IT infrastructure—it's transforming *everything*. "Not only do we have to change the infrastructure; we have to fundamentally change the way we build applications," says Bullotta. "Hundreds of millions of new applications will be built. Some of them will be very small, and very transient. Traditional IT organizations—along with their tooling, approaches, and processes—will have to change. For IT, it's going to be a different world. We're seeing the 'API-ification' of the enterprise."

Traditional software development cycles taking three to 18 months (or even longer) are simply not rapid enough for businesses competing in 21st-century markets. "Things are happening too fast, and the traditional approach isn't feasible," says Bullotta. "IT isn't set up for handling lots of small projects. Costs and overhead kill the ROI." Traditional IT tends to focus on completing two or three multimillion-dollar projects annually. "Think of all the opportunities that are lost. Imagine instead doing a thousand smaller projects, each delivering a 300 percent ROI. They would generate an enormous amount of money," says Bullotta.

The key, according to Bullotta, is "ubiquitous connectivity," which is a diplomatic way of saying that many parts of the enterprise still don't communicate or share information effectively. The lack of sharing suggests there is still a need for practical, real-time collaboration systems. Dozens of vendors offer collaboration tools, but it's hard to find companies that use them systematically.

The idea that critical information is still trapped in silos echoes throughout conversations about the impact of big data on enterprise IT. Sometimes it almost seems as though everyone in the world *except IT* intuitively grasps the underlying risks and benefits of big data. Or can it be that IT is actively resisting the transformational aspects of big data out of irrational fears that big data will somehow upset longstanding relationships with big vendors like IBM, Microsoft, and Oracle?

Beyond Infrastructure

William Ruh is chief digital officer of GE Software (*https://www.gesoftware.com/*). Before joining up with GE, he was a vice president at Cisco, where he was responsible for developing advanced services and solutions. He operates at the bleeding edge, trying to figure out practical ways for commercializing new technologies at a global scale. When you're on the phone with Ruh, you feel like you're chatting with an astronaut on the International Space Station or a deep-sea diver exploring the wreckage of a long-lost ship.

From Ruh's perspective, transforming IT infrastructure is only part of the story. "I think we all understand there's a great opportunity here. But it's not just about IT. This is really where IT meets OT—operational technology. OT is going to ride the new IT infrastructure," he says.

IT is for the enterprise; OT is for the physical world of interconnected smart machines. "Machines can be very chatty," says Ruh. "You'll have all of those machines, chatting among themselves in the cloud, pushing out patches and fixes, synchronizing and updating themselves—it will be asset management on steroids."

In the world of OT, there is no downtime. Everything runs 24/7, continuously, 365 days a year. "People get irritated when their Internet goes down, but they get extraordinarily upset when their electricity fails," says Ruh. The role of OT is making sure that the real world keeps running, even when your cell phone drops a call or your streaming video is momentarily interrupted.

OT is enabled by the Industrial Internet, which is GE's name for the Internet of Things. Unlike the Internet of Things, which sounds almost comical, the Industrial Internet suggests something more like the Industrial Revolution. It evokes images of a looming transformation that's big, scary, and permanent.

That kind of transformation would not necessarily be bad. Given the choice, most of us would take the 21st century over the 18th century any day. There will be broad economic benefits, too. GE estimates the "wave of innovation" accompanying the Industrial

Internet "could boost global GDP by as much as $10–15 trillion over the next 20 years, through accelerated productivity growth." IDC projects the trend will generate in the neighborhood of $9 trillion in annual sales by the end of the decade. On the low end, Gartner predicts a measly $1.9 trillion in sales and cost savings over the same period.[1]

Economic incentives, whether real or imagined, will drive the next wave of IT transformation. It's important to remember that during the Industrial Revolution, factory owners didn't buy steam engines because they thought they were "cool." They bought them because they did the math and realized that in the long run, it made more economic sense to invest in steam power than in draft animals (horses, oxen, etc.), watermills, and windmills.

Not everyone is certain that IT is prepared for transformation on a scale that's similar to the Industrial Revolution. In addition to delivering service with near-zero latency and near-zero downtime, IT will be expected to handle a whole new galaxy of security threats. "When everything is connected, it ups the ante in the cybersecurity game," says Ruh. "It's bad enough when people hack your information. It will be worse when people hack your physical devices. The way that IT thinks about security has to change. We can't go with the old philosophy in the new world we're building."

Can We Handle the Truth?

If problems such as latency, downtime, and security aren't daunting enough, Mike Marcotte offers another challenge for data-driven organizations: dealing with the truth, or more specifically, dealing with the sought-after Holy Grail of data management, the "single version of the truth."

Marcotte is the chief digital officer at EchoStar, a global provider of satellite operations and video delivery solutions. A winner of multiple Emmy Awards, the company has pioneered advancements in the set-top box and satellite industries, and significantly influenced the way consumers view, receive, and manage TV programming.

---

1 For an excellent overview, read Steve Johnson's article in the *San Jose Mercury News*, "The 'Internet of Things' Could Be the Next Industrial Revolution." (*http://bit.ly/NLdtcL*)

As a seasoned and experienced IT executive, Marcotte finds the cultural challenges of new infrastructure more interesting than the technical issues. "The IT systems are fully baked at this point. The infrastructure and architecture required to collect and analyze massive amounts of data work phenomenally well. The real challenge is getting people to agree on which data is the right data," says Marcotte.

The old legacy IT systems allowed each line of business to bring its own version of the truth to the table. Each business unit generated a unique set of data, and it was difficult to dispute the veracity of someone else's numbers. Newer data management systems, running on modern enterprise infrastructure, deliver one set of numbers, eliminate many of the fudge factors, and present something much closer to the raw truth. "In the past, you could have 200 versions of the truth. Now the architecture and the computing platforms are so good that you can have a single version of the truth. In many companies, that will open up a real can of worms," he says.

In a tense moment near the end of *A Few Good Men*, the commanding officer played by Jack Nicholson snarls, "You can't handle the truth!" Was he right? Can we handle the truth, or will it prove too much for us? Driven by the growth of big data, is our new IT infrastructure the path to a better world, or a Pandora's Box? The prospects are certainly exciting, if not downright sexy.

CHAPTER 4

When Hardware Meets Software

Topline Summary

Until recently, the term "smart machines" evoked thoughts of R2-D2, HAL, or the Terminator. Today, we're more likely to think of thermostats, wearable fitness trackers, and automobiles. Hardware and software have moved closer together, blurring the lines that traditionally separated developers, designers, manufacturers, and users.

This report, written in the spring of 2014, describes how the Internet of Things, 3D printing, and the Maker Movement are transforming the world of product development and laying the foundation for a new generation of "indie" manufacturers and tech startups.

Welcome to the Age of Indie Hardware

In the Internet of Things, what's old is new, and what's new happens much faster.

When most of us first caught up with the Internet, it seemed like a magical door to a virtual reality played out in the infinite reaches of cyberspace. Today, it seems as though everyone is talking about the Internet in terms of its ability to get things done in the physical world of meat and machinery. We hear people talking about the Internet of Things, the Industrial Internet, and the Internet of Everything.

Is the Internet a wonderful rabbit hole into the infinite mind of the cosmos or the unsexy front end of a new industrial age? As Al Pacino puts it so eloquently in *The Godfather Part III*, "Just when I thought I was out, they pull me back in."

For those of us in the trenches of the Internet counterrevolution, the apparent shift in interest from virtual to physical benefits translates to a blurring of the boundaries between software and hardware. In a global economy driven by consumer technologies, software developers need to think more like product designers, and product designers need to think more like software developers.

Until relatively recently, there was no bright-line demarcation between "hardware people" and "software people." Techies were techies, and everyone who was interested in electronics learned how to read a circuit diagram and use a soldering iron.

The rise of programmable computers spawned a new kind of techie —the software engineer. Each twist and turn of the modern industrial economy leads to increasing specialization. Technology was not exempt from this rule, and soon enough you had software developers who had never seen a finished product roll off an assembly line.

All trends rise and fall. A new generation of smart techies has emerged to challenge the false duality of the hardware versus software paradigm. The spiritual heirs of the ham radio operators and homemade rocket enthusiasts of the 1940s and 50s have coalesced to form a maker culture that is quietly subverting the standard industrial model of product design and development.

Even if they aren't the actual grandsons and granddaughters of the original hobbyists, they apply the same kind of grit, smarts, and do-it-yourself confidence as earlier generations of inventors and tinkerers who labored in basements, backyards, and garages all over the world.

Unlike their predecessors, whose audiences were limited mostly to friends and family members, the new generation is sharing its inventiveness globally and selling gadgets through maker-friendly e-commerce markets such as Tindie, Make:, and Grand St.

"We're increasingly seeing people who are able to support themselves—or who at least are close to supporting themselves—by selling technology they've created," says Julia Grace, head of engineering at Tindie. "Most of our sellers are people who started off as hobbyists, doing this on nights and weekends. As demand has grown, however, and as our sellers gain access to facilities and manufacturing techniques that were previously available only to people working in large companies, they're able to produce their items faster and sell more of them."

Grace compares indie hardware markets like Tindie to Etsy, the successful e-commerce website specializing in handmade artisanal products. On Etsy, you can shop for handcrafted ceramics and jewelry; on Tindie you can shop for a Doomsday Clock Shield with Rotary Encoder, or Tapster, a robot designed to play Angry Birds.

Indeed, Tapster is one of indie hardware's major success stories. Designed originally for gamers, it's been upgraded and adopted by large manufacturers as a low-cost machine for testing mobile apps.

Tapster was invented by Jason Huggins, a software developer who uses open source hardware technology such as Bitbeam, a modular building system similar to Lego Technic. What's especially interesting about Bitbeam is that it can be made with a 3D printer—which means, of course, that it is potentially scalable. When something works and can be produced in large numbers easily, watch out.

For the moment, much of what's made by the maker community is consumed largely by other makers. But the winds of change are blowing. If a handful of visionary Fortune 500 firms are using Tapster, more will surely follow in their footsteps tomorrow.

Two or three years from now, Tapster (or something like it) might be seen in retrospect as the Altair 8800 of the indie manufacturing era. If that's the case, then the Commodore 64 and Apple I of the new era are already in the wings and waiting for their cue to take the stage.

It's also quite possible that the next cool thing produced by the indie manufacturing culture won't be a computer. Grand St., launched in late 2012, is also an online market for nifty products based on cutting-edge tech. In addition to providing a market for sellers, it serves as a platform for design and development.

"We offer three types of products," explains Amanda Peyton, Grand St.'s CEO and cofounder. "First, we have a traditional marketplace for products that are finished and ready to ship. Second, we have a 'beta' marketplace for products from makers who want feedback from people who aren't friends and family. Third, we have a preorder marketplace for products that aren't ready for shipping, but will likely ship in the next six months. It's a way to test demand for a product before it hits the market. Sometimes there's an actual prototype and sometimes there's just a rendering."

Grand St.'s model offers potential consumers a view into the previously hidden universe of product design and development. In a very real sense, Grand St. pulls back the curtain, creating transparency in a process that is usually shrouded in secrecy.

The new approach isn't just about lifting the veil and showing consumers how it all works. It's based on shifting economics. "The capital requirements around product development have really changed," says Peyton. "Previously, you needed lots of money up front to fund an entire product development process. Now you can engage with your audience much earlier, and you can forecast the demand for products before they've hit the market."[1]

In the world of consumer electronics, for example, the impact of this new approach means that smaller teams—and fewer resources—are required for launching new products. When you need only a couple of designers and developers working on a project, time-to-market cycles can be compressed dramatically. More important, you don't need to raise gazillions in fresh capital to set up an assembly line.

Mindset and Culture

Julia Grace grew up playing first-generation Nintendo games. Her first computer was a used Commodore 64, and she learned programming from books she found at the public library. In today's world of ubiquitous broadband connectivity and instant streaming, that makes her seem very "old school." But her background and mindset are typical of the maker movement, which is essentially a 21st-century variation on the pioneer cultures that stressed self-sufficiency and self-reliance in the 19th-century.

---

1 In April 2014, after Amanda Peyton was interviewed for this report, Grand St. announced that it would be acquired by Etsy. "While this is a big step for us as a company, we plan to change very little about the site and your experience of Grand St. in the near term," Amanda Peyton wrote on her blog. "We exist to bring you the best in indie electronics from designers and makers all over the world, and we'll continue to do that at grandst.com. We will continue to launch new features and have a few coming out soon that we think you'll love."

It's fair to say that not everyone shares the retro mindset and passionate enthusiasm for handcrafted small-batch technologies. A quick tour of any college dormitory reveals a startling lack of interest in any kind of technology that can't be assembled intuitively, immediately, and without any tools. When was the last time you saw a college student with a soldering iron, wire strippers, or a circuit tester?

The phenomenon doesn't merely apply to geeks and nerds. In the 1950s, you couldn't drive two blocks without seeing someone working on a souped-up car with a customized chrome-plated exhaust system, tuck-and-roll leather upholstery, and an engine hood modified to accommodate a big nasty turbo charger. If you want to see the modern-day equivalent of 20th-century gearheads, you must travel to Shenzhen, a large city in China's Guangdong Province, just north of Hong Kong.

Tigers Pacing in a Cage

Andrew "bunnie" Huang has a Ph.D. in electrical engineering from MIT, but he is most famous for reverse-engineering the Xbox, establishing his reputation as one of the world's greatest hardware hackers. He sees an evolving relationship between hardware and software.

"It used to be that products were limited solely by the capability of their hardware. Early radios, for example, had mechanical buttons that acted directly on the physics of the receiver," says Huang. "As hardware becomes more capable, the user experience of the hardware is more dictated by the software that runs on it. Now that hardware is ridiculously capable—you basically have supercomputers in your pockets that cost next to nothing—pretty much the entire user experience of the product is dictated by the software. The hardware simply serves as an elusive constraint on the user experience."

Hardware is "a cage," says Huang, and good software developers learn to work within the constraints of the hardware. "When I work with programmers on new products, I take the first prototype, put it on the desk, and I say, 'Welcome to your new cage.' That's the reality. There's a hard wall. But we try to build the cage big enough so there are options for programmers. A quad-core Android phone with a gigabyte of memory is a pretty big cage. Sometimes when programmers feel constrained, they're just being lazy. There's always more than one way to skin a cat in the software world."

For instance, if battery life is an issue—and when isn't it?—a programmer has a multitude of tools to optimize for power consumption: she can reduce CPU clock speed or shut down subsystems when the device is idling; she can optimize popular libraries and routines to take less energy to compute; or she can preload or precompute data images so energy consumption is shifted to the cloud.

Even the highest-level UI decisions impact battery life; an animated home-screen wallpaper will burn batteries faster than a static background. On the other hand, no phone will ever contain a battery with the energy density required to brew a full pot of coffee.

While it seems unlikely that consumers will demand phones that also brew coffee, software designers routinely face challenging constraints, such as writing code for the embedded processors in low-end consumer products. These systems contain smaller CPUs and as little as a few dozen kilobytes of memory. "That's when you see programmers pacing around like tigers in a cage," says Huang.

From Huang's perspective, the introduction and rapid proliferation of multitouch input digitizers on user interfaces (think of any smartphone screen) has had the greatest impact on the relationship between hardware and software. "Before that, and without that, the experience of that product would have been not nearly as interesting. The pinch zoom, the whole scrolling action that we are now very familiar with, was very revolutionary. They redesigned the whole user experience around that input sensor," says Huang.

Certainly, one of the most compelling features of the iPhone was its touch screen. Most of the same tasks could be performed with buttons or a stylus, but the user experience was so completely different that the input digitizer became an indisputable competitive advantage. At the same moment that it became something everyone wanted, it also became the new cage.

But that's the nature of product design. Yesterday it was novel, today it's standard, and tomorrow it feels old-fashioned. Designers and developers can curse at the whims of temperamental consumers, but they cannot ignore them.

"I've run into developers who make inaccurate assumptions about hardware and who start complaining loudly about the design of the hardware when they bump into problems," says Huang. "They want you to loosen the constraints. But it always boils down to cost. You can do anything, but it will cost you money. Then the company will tell you they can't sell the product at a higher price point."

Occasionally, says bunnie, he meets developers who are "truly proactive in thinking through the whole process. But it's rare to find people with the skills required to develop products that are great from front to back."

Understanding the interplay between software, hardware, and the existing supply chain is important, he says. And that's why many companies are heading to Shenzhen—because it's one of the few places in the world where there is a critical mass of people with the multiple skill sets required for meeting the endless demands of a growing global consumer economy that constantly hungers for exciting new products.

The stalls, booths, shops, and mini-factories of Shenzhen are filled with younger and even scrappier versions of bunnie, and they are all looking for the big break that will elevate them into the spotlight. You might not find someone to refit your '55 Chevy Bel Air with an air intake, but if you're looking for someone to customize your smartphone, you've come to the right place.

Hardware Wars

Joichi Ito is the director of the MIT Media Lab.[2] Ito recalls sending a group of MIT students to Shenzhen so they could see for themselves how manufacturing is evolving. "Once they got their heads around the processes in a deep way, they understood the huge differences between prototyping and manufacturing. Design for prototyping and design for manufacturing are fundamentally different," says Ito. The problem in today's world, according to Ito, is that "we have abstracted industrial design to the point where we think that we can just throw designs over a wall," and somehow they will magically reappear as finished products.

The trip to Shenzhen helped the students understand the manufacturing process from start to finish. "In Shenzhen, they have a $12

---

2 Joichi Ito is also cochair of the upcoming O'Reilly Solid Conference (*http://solid con.com*).

phone. It's amazing. It has no screws holding it together. It's clearly designed to be as cheap as possible. It's also clearly designed by someone who really understands manufacturing *and* understands what consumers want."

Ito also sees a significant difference between what's happening on the factory floors in Shenzhen and the maker movement. "We're not talking about low-volume, DIY manufacturing," he says. Instead, Ito's students are working through the problems and challenges of a real, live paradigm shift—the kind of gut-wrenching upheaval described in Thomas S. Kuhn's seminal book, *The Structure of Scientific Revolutions* (University of Chicago Press).

From Kuhn's point of view, a paradigm shift isn't a cause for celebration or blithe headlines—it's a sharp and unexpected blow that topples old theories, wrecks careers, and sweeps aside entire fields of knowledge.

The existing paradigm—the status quo—favors companies whose products and services are based mainly on software, because software can be scaled rapidly at minimal cost. The emerging paradigm favors companies whose products and services are based mainly on hardware, because the cost of developing and manufacturing hardware is dropping precipitously.

Software and Moore's law go together like soup and sandwiches. Put less kindly, software made Moore's law look like a real law. Hardware is a different kettle of fish, since it involves orchestrating and synchronizing dozens (and sometimes hundreds) of complex interlocking processes, such as product design, prototyping, sourcing raw materials, managing supply chains, setting up assembly lines, building or leasing factories, setting up distribution channels, packaging, shipping, and much more.

The innovators in places like Shenzhen are showing the world that hardware startups can look a lot like software startups. They don't necessarily need tons of seed money or venture capital, they can be spun up relatively quickly, and if they fail, they can be broken down and sold for spare parts. That's the paradigm shift—and the people who control large portions of the global economy and decide where to invest trillions of dollars, yen, yuan, won, or rupees are beginning to see hardware as the coolest new shiny object.

Does This Mean I Need to Buy a Lathe?

The Internet of Things doesn't presage a return to the world of smoke-belching factories and floors covered with sawdust. But it does signify that change is afoot for any business or activity related to the information technology or communications industries.

"Not everyone will become a hardware designer," says Ito. But many students, software engineers, and entrepreneurs will see the advantages of learning how to work with hardware. "It's never too late to learn this stuff," says Ito, "if you decide that you want to do it."

At minimum, software engineers should learn as much about design and manufacturing as possible. "Buy an Arduino[3] and start building. Everything you need to learn is on the Web," urges Jordan Husney.

In the same way that software people will have to reconfigure their modes of thinking, hardware people will need to learn new technical skills and new ways of looking at problems, says Husney. "They will have to become more comfortable with uncertainty occurring later and later in the process," he says. "Hardware engineers will keep things in the realm of bits (as opposed to committing them to atoms) by sharing designs using digital collaboration and simulation tools virtually, while testing multiple physical prototypes. I think we're going to see the supply chain start to shift around these concepts."

The idea of rapid and continuous iteration (some prefer to call it "continuous improvement") dovetails with the notion that designers will have to become accustomed to higher levels of uncertainty farther into the manufacturing process. "It used to be that you'd ship a product and it was considered finished. Now, folks are shipping beta products (with unfinished hardware and software) to gather more feedback from the field," says Husney. "We're seeing this with Coin [a startup with a card-like device that stores information about the credit cards you carry in your wallet] and Energy Aware, which has just begun shipping its beta whole-home energy monitors."

---

3 According to its home page, "Arduino is an open source electronics prototyping platform based on flexible, easy-to-use hardware and software. It's intended for artists, designers, hobbyists, and anyone interested in creating interactive objects or environments."

Designers now see their products as platforms, says Husney. "With remote connectivity and remote updates, they're able to iterate and add value to products that their customers already own. My iPhone, for example, gets better every day. Apple continuously produces new operating system enhancements and adds new functionality. The app platform allows software makers to increase the value of the hardware in my pocket."

Obstacles, Hurdles, and Brighter Street Lighting

More than one observer has noted that while it's relatively easy for consumers to communicate directly with their smart devices, it's still quite difficult for smart devices to communicate directly, or even indirectly, with each other. William Ruh, chief digital officer of GE Software, drives the company's efforts to construct an Industrial Internet that will enable devices large and small to chat freely among themselves, automatically and autonomously.

Ruh is the opposite of a mad scientist. From his perspective, the Industrial Internet is a benign platform for helping the world become a quieter, calmer, and less dangerous place.

"In the past, hardware existed without software. You think about the founding of GE and the invention of the lightbulb—you turned it on and you turned it off. Zero lines of code. Today we have street lighting systems with mesh networks and 20 million lines of code," says Ruh. "Machines used to be completely mechanical. Today they are part digital. Software is part of the hardware. That opens up huge possibilities."

A hundred years ago, street lighting was an on-or-off affair. In the future, when a crime is committed at night, a police officer could raise the intensity of the nearby street lights by tapping a smartphone app. This would create near-daylight conditions around a crime scene, and hopefully make it harder for the perpetrators to escape unseen. "Our machines are becoming much more intelligent. With software embedded in them, they're becoming brilliant," says Ruh.

But the Internet we've grown accustomed to isn't reliable, robust, or antifragile enough for what Ruh envisions, which is a world of smart devices that are constantly sharing data and making real-time decisions.

Networks of smart devices already exist in the aviation industry. The locomotives and wind turbines GE builds have smart components that report their status and warn of impending breakdowns. The rest of the world, however, gets by on an Internet designed mostly for sharing noncritical information.

For example, if your Internet connection goes down while you're sending an email to a friend, posting a status update on Facebook, or watching someone's cat riding a Roomba vacuum on YouTube, it's not a big deal. Almost all of the technology we associate with our PCs and mobile devices is consumer technology, which means that it's reasonably OK but not the absolute best it can be. And for 99.9 percent of what we do in our daily lives, that's fine. Even the dreaded "blue screen of death" wasn't really fatal.

All of that changes when the machines we depend on for matters of life and death are added to the mix. When jet engines, municipal water systems, and heart-lung machines join the conversation, we need an Internet (and all of the information and communication technologies supporting it) that performs flawlessly, every second of every day. Today, when your LinkedIn page freezes, it's irritating, but not dangerous. Tomorrow, when your Google driverless car freezes (let's not use the word "crash"), it's a different story.

As a culture, we're going to have to figure out how to make hardware that works all the time. "People get testy when their cell phone drops a call, but they get *really* testy when their electricity stops working," says Ruh. When lives are at stake, concepts such as reliability, scalability, and security become incredibly relevant. They become more than just buzzwords used by marketers and industry journalists.

"We have a visceral response when the machines we depend on stop working. We expect the software in our machines to be as good as the hardware. Meeting those expectations requires a different approach to software design, a different mentality," says Ruh.

The "old" mentality, says Ruh, meant designing products for "rocket scientists" and assuming that they would eventually, through trial and error, figure out how to use it. As a result, most products had features that people never used. Microsoft Word is the classic example of the "old" software design mentality, and it's probably fair to say that most flat-screen televisions are shipped with more features than will ever be used by the typical consumer. Earlier in this paper, Joichi Ito spoke of throwing a design over a wall and expecting someone on the other side to turn it into a finished product. Ruh offers a similar thought, suggesting that many software designers neglect to consider the consequences of their designs on the end user. He predicts that more companies will require designers to come up with "zero installation time" products and services that work right out of the box, requiring no setup or fiddling to deliver expected levels of performance.

"People today assume they have a certain set of inalienable rights, such as the right to see water flowing when they turn on the tap and the right to see the lights go on when they touch a switch. People feel very strongly about those rights and they will get upset when they feel that their basic needs aren't met," says Ruh.

Is the Industrial Internet—the Internet of Things, the Internet of Everything—prepared to deliver that kind of service? Are products designed for the new age of smart devices capable of delivering on expectations such as continuous improvement, 24/7 reliability, and zero installation?

In a new book, *The Zero Marginal Cost Society: The Internet of Things, The Collaborative Commons, and The Eclipse of Capitalism* (*http://amzn.to/1L0Kiiy*) (Palgrave Macmillan), author Jeremy Rifkin notes that in 2007, "there were 10 million sensors connecting every type of human contrivance to the Internet of Things. In 2013, that number was set to exceed 3.5 billion, and even more impressive, by 2030 it is projected that 100 trillion sensors will connect to the IoT."

It seems highly unlikely that the Internet—which was neither conceived nor designed to function as an industrial-strength communications system—will ever fulfill the role of a universal medium for connecting everything to everything. What seems more likely, however, is that machines will become smarter and more autonomous. We will design machines that we can trust to do the right thing, even when we're not keeping an eye on them.

The concept of trustable machines returns us to our earlier conversation about the evolving relationships between software and hardware, and between design and manufacturing. Ideas such as "zero installation time," "zero user interface," and "invisible buttons" require ditching the old paradigms of software versus hardware and design versus manufacturing. As we become increasingly dependent on our gadgets and devices, our primary concerns will narrow down to safety, reliability, redundancy, and survivability. In a world of brilliant machines and 100 trillion networked sensors, the main question will be, "Does this thing actually work?"

CHAPTER 5

Real-Time Big Data Analytics

Topline Summary

How fast is fast? Are you looking at "real time" from the perspective of a human or a machine? Is there a "time barrier" that puts an upper limit on the efficiency of big data analytics? Those are just a few of the questions keeping data scientists awake at night.

This report, written in late 2012 and early 2013, describes the layers and components of the emerging real-time big data analytics stack, and sketches out the architectures required for applying data science routinely in the real world.

Oceans of Data, Grains of Time

Imagine that it's 2007. You're a top executive at a major search engine company, and Steve Jobs has just unveiled the iPhone. You immediately ask yourself, "Should we shift resources away from some of our current projects so we can create an experience expressly for iPhone users?" Then you begin wondering, "What if it's all hype? Steve is a great showman...how can we predict if the iPhone is a fad or the next big thing?"

The good news is that you've got plenty of data at your disposal. The bad news is that you have no way of querying that data and discovering the answer to a critical question: How many people are accessing my sites from their iPhones?

Back in 2007, you couldn't even ask the question without upgrading the schema in your data warehouse, an expensive process that might have taken two months. Your only choice was to wait and hope that a competitor didn't eat your lunch in the meantime.

Justin Erickson, a senior product manager at Cloudera, told me a version of that story and I want to share it with you because it neatly illustrates the difference between traditional analytics and real-time big data analytics. Back then, you had to know the kinds of questions you planned to ask before you stored your data.

"Fast-forward to the present, and technologies like Hadoop (*http:// hadoop.apache.org/*) give you the scale and flexibility to store data before you know how you are going to process it," says Erickson. "Technologies such as MapReduce (*http://en.wikipedia.org/wiki/ MapReduce*), Hive (*http://hive.apache.org/*), and Impala (*http:// bit.ly/impaladoc*) enable you to run queries without changing the data structures underneath."

Today, you are much less likely to face a scenario in which you cannot query data and get a response back in a brief period of time. Analytical processes that used to require months, days, or hours have been reduced to minutes, seconds, and fractions of seconds.

But shorter processing times have led to higher expectations. Two years ago, many data analysts thought that generating a result from a query in less than 40 minutes was nothing short of miraculous. Today, they expect to see results in under a minute. That's practically the speed of thought—you think of a query, you get a result, and you begin your experiment.

"It's about moving with greater speed toward previously unknown questions, defining new insights, and reducing the time between when an event happens somewhere in the world and someone responds or reacts to that event," says Erickson.

A rapidly emerging universe of newer technologies has dramatically reduced data processing cycle time, making it possible to explore and experiment with data in ways that would not have been practical or even possible a few years ago.

Despite the availability of new tools and systems for handling massive amounts of data at incredible speeds, however, the real promise of advanced data analytics lies beyond the realm of pure technology.

"Real-time big data isn't just a process for storing petabytes or exabytes of data in a data warehouse," says Michael Minelli, coauthor of *Big Data, Big Analytics* (*http://amzn.to/1xAf89m*) (Wiley). "It's about the ability to make better decisions and take meaningful actions at the right time. It's about detecting fraud while someone is swiping a credit card, or triggering an offer while a shopper is standing in a checkout line, or placing an ad on a website while someone is reading a specific article. It's about combining and analyzing data so you can take the right action, at the right time, and at the right place."

For some, real-time big data analytics (RTBDA) is a ticket to improved sales, higher profits, and lower marketing costs. To others, it signals the dawn of a new era in which machines begin to think and respond more like humans.

How Fast Is Fast?

The capability to store data quickly isn't new. What's new is the capability to do something meaningful with that data, quickly and cost-effectively. Businesses and governments have been storing huge amounts of data for decades. What we are witnessing now, however, is an explosion of new techniques for analyzing those large data sets. In addition to new capabilities for handling large amounts of data, we're also seeing a proliferation of new technologies designed to handle complex, nontraditional data—precisely the kinds of unstructured or semi-structured data generated by social media, mobile communications, customer service records, warranties, census reports, sensors, and web logs. In the past, data had to be arranged neatly in tables. In today's world of data analytics, anything goes. Heterogeneity is the new normal, and modern data scientists are accustomed to hacking their way through tangled clumps of messy data culled from multiple sources.

Software frameworks such as Hadoop and MapReduce, which support distributed processing applications across relatively inexpensive commodity hardware, now make it possible to mix and match data from many disparate sources. Today's data sets aren't merely larger than the older data sets—they're significantly more complex.

"Big data has three dimensions—volume, variety, and velocity," says Minelli. "And within each of those three dimensions is a wide range of variables."

The ability to manage large and complex sets of data hasn't diminished the appetite for more size and greater speed. Every day it seems that a new technique or application is introduced that pushes the edges of the speed-size envelope even further.

Druid (*http://metamarkets.com/druid/*), for example, is a system for scanning tens of billions of records per second. It boasts scan speeds of 33 million rows/second/core and ingest speeds of 10 thousand records/second/node. It can query 6 terabytes of in-memory data in 1.4 seconds. As Eric Tschetter wrote in his blog (*http://metamarkets.com/2012/scaling-druid/*), Druid has "the power to move planetary-size data sets with speed."

When systems operate at such blinding velocities, it seems odd to quibble over a few milliseconds here or there. But Ted Dunning, an architect at MapR Technologies, raises a concern worth noting. "Many of the terms used by people are confusing. Some of the definitions are what I would call *squishy*. They don't say, *If this takes longer than 2.3 seconds, we're out.* Google, for instance, definitely wants their system to be as fast as possible and they definitely put real-time constraints on the internals of their system to make sure that it gives up on certain approaches very quickly. But overall, the system itself is not real time. It's pretty fast, almost all the time. That's what I mean by a *squishy* definition of real time."

The difference between a hard definition and a "squishy" definition isn't merely semantic—it has real-world consequences. For example, many people don't understand that real-time online algorithms are constrained by time and space limitations. If you "unbound" them to allow more data, they can no longer function as real-time algorithms. "People need to begin developing an intuition about which kinds of processing are bounded in time, and which kinds aren't," says Dunning. For example, algorithms that keep unique identifiers of visitors to a website can break down if traffic suddenly increases. Algorithms designed to prevent the same email from being re-sent within seven days through a system work well until the scale of the system expands radically.

The Apache Drill project (*http://incubator.apache.org/drill/*) will address the "squishy" factor by scanning through smaller sets of data very quickly. Drill is the open source cousin of Dremel (*http://bit.ly/dremel-engine*), a Google tool that rips through larger data sets at blazing speeds and spits out summary results, sidestepping the scale issue.

Dunning is one of the Drill project's core developers. He sees Drill as complementary to existing frameworks such as Hadoop. Drill brings big data analytics a step closer to real-time interactive processing, which is definitely a step in the right direction.

"Drill takes a slightly different tack than Dremel," says Dunning. "Drill is trying to be more things to more people—probably at the cost of some performance, but that's just mostly due to the different environment. Google is a well-controlled, very well-managed data environment. But the outside world is a messy place. Nobody is in charge. Data appears in all kinds of ways, and people have all kinds of preferences for how they want to express what they want, and what kinds of languages they want to write their queries in."

Dunning notes that both Drill and Dremel scan data in parallel. "Using a variety of online algorithms, they're able to complete scans —doing filtering operations, doing aggregates, and so on—in a parallel way, in a fairly short amount of time. But they basically scan the whole table. They are both full-table scan tools that perform good aggregation, good sorting, and good *top 40* sorts of measurements."

In many situations involving big data, random failures and resulting data loss can become issues. "If I'm bringing data in from many different systems, data loss could skew my analysis pretty dramatically," says Cloudera's Erickson. "When you have lots of data moving across multiple networks and many machines, there's a greater chance that something will break and portions of the data won't be available."

Cloudera has addressed those problems by creating a system of tools, including Flume (*https://github.com/cloudera/flume*) and SQOOP (*https://github.com/cloudera/sqoop*), which handle ingestion from multiple sources into Hadoop, and Impala, which enables real-time, ad hoc querying of data.

"Before Imapala, you did the machine learning and larger-scale processes in Hadoop, and the ad hoc analysis in Hive, which involves relatively slow batch processing," says Erickson. "Alternatively, you can perform the ad hoc analysis against a traditional database system, which limits your ad hoc exploration to the data that is captured and loaded into the predefined schema. So essentially you are doing machine learning on one side, ad hoc querying on the other side, and then correlating the data between the two systems."

Impala, says Erickson, enables ad hoc SQL analysis "directly on top of your big data systems. You don't have to define the schema before you load the data."

For example, let's say you're a large financial services institution. Obviously, you're going to be on the lookout for credit card fraud. Some kinds of fraud are relatively easy to spot. If a cardholder makes a purchase in Philadelphia and another purchase 10 minutes later in San Diego, a fraud alert is triggered. But other kinds of credit card fraud involve numerous small purchases, across multiple accounts, over long time periods.

Finding those kinds of fraud requires different analytical approaches. If you are running traditional analytics on top of a traditional enterprise data warehouse, it's going to take you longer to recognize and respond to new kinds of fraud than it would if you had the capabilities to run ad hoc queries in real time. When you're dealing with fraud, every lost minute translates into lost money.

How Real Is Real Time?

Here's another complication: The meaning of "real time" can vary depending on the context in which it is used.

"In the same sense that there really is no such thing as truly unstructured data, there's no such thing as real time. There's only near-real time," says John Akred, a senior manager within the data domain of Accenture's Emerging Technology Innovations group. "Typically when we're talking about real-time or near real-time systems, what we mean is architectures that allow you to respond to data as you receive it without necessarily persisting it to a database first."

In other words, real-time denotes the ability to process data as it arrives, rather than storing the data and retrieving it at some point in the future. That's the primary significance of the term—real-time means that you're processing data in the present, rather than in the future.

But "the present" also has different meanings to different users. From the perspective of an online merchant, "the present" means the attention span of a potential customer. If the processing time of a transaction exceeds the customer's attention span, the merchant doesn't consider it real time.

From the perspective of an options trader, however, real time means milliseconds. From the perspective of a guided missile, real time means microseconds.

For most data analysts, real time means "pretty fast" at the data layer and "very fast" at the decision layer. "Real time is for robots," says Joseph Hellerstein, chancellor's professor of computer science at UC Berkeley. "If you have people in the loop, it's not real time. Most people take a second or two to react, and that's plenty of time for a traditional transactional system to handle input and output."

That doesn't mean that developers have abandoned the quest for speed. Supported by a Google grant, Matei Zaharia is working on his Ph.D. at UC Berkeley. He is an author of Spark (*http://spark-project.org*), an open source cluster computing system that can be programmed quickly and runs fast. Spark relies on "resilient distributed data sets" (RDDs) and "can be used to interactively query 1 to 2 terabytes of data in less than a second."

In scenarios involving machine learning algorithms and other multipass analytics algorithms, "Spark can run 10× to 100× faster than Hadoop MapReduce," says Zaharia. Spark is also the engine behind Shark (*http://shark.cs.berkeley.edu*), a data warehousing system.

According to Zaharia, companies such as Conviva and Quantifind have written UIs that launch Spark on the back end of analytics dashboards. "You see the statistics on a dashboard, and if you're wondering about some data that hasn't been computed, you can ask a question that goes out to a parallel computation on Spark and you get back an answer in about half a second."

Storm (*http://storm-project.net*) is an open source low-latency stream processing system designed to integrate with existing queuing and bandwidth systems. It is used by companies such as Twitter, the Weather Channel, Groupon, and Ooyala. Nathan Marz, lead engineer at BackType (acquired by Twitter in 2011), is the author of Storm and other open source projects such as Cascalog (*http://bit.ly/1Mq0zdZ*) and ElephantDB (*http://bit.ly/1KPi3RV*).

"There are really only two paradigms for data processing: batch and stream," says Marz. "Batch processing is fundamentally high-latency. So if you're trying to look at a terabyte of data all at once, you'll never be able to do that computation in less than a second with batch processing."

Stream processing looks at smaller amounts of data as they arrive. "You can do intense computations, like parallel search, and merge queries on the fly," says Marz. "Normally, if you want to do a search query, you need to create search indexes, which can be a slow process on one machine. With Storm, you can stream the process across many machines, and get much quicker results."

Twitter uses Storm to identify trends in near real time. Ideally, says Marz, Storm will also enable Twitter to "understand someone's intent in virtually real time. For example, let's say that someone tweets that he's going snowboarding. Storm would help you figure out which ad would be most appropriate for that person, at just the right time."

Storm is also relatively user friendly. "People love Storm because it's easy to use. It solves really hard problems such as fault tolerance and dealing with partial failures in distributed processing. We have a platform you can build on. You don't have to focus on the infrastructure because that work has already been done. You can set up Storm by yourself and have it running in minutes," says Marz.

The RTBDA Stack

At this moment, it's clear that an architecture for handling RTBDA is slowly emerging from a disparate set of programs and tools. What isn't clear, however, is what that architecture will look like. One goal of this paper is sketching out a practical RTBDA roadmap that will serve a variety of stakeholders including users, vendors, investors, and corporate executives such as CIOs, CFOs, and COOs who make or influence purchasing decisions around information technology.

Focusing on the stakeholders and their needs is important because it reminds us that the RTBDA technology exists for a specific purpose: creating value from data. It is also important to remember that "value" and "real time" will suggest different meanings to different subsets of stakeholders. There is presently no one-size-fits-all model, which makes sense when you consider that the interrelationships among people, processes, and technologies within the RTBDA universe are still evolving.

David Smith writes a popular blog (*http://blog.revolutionanalyt ics.com*) for Revolution Analytics on open source R, a programming language designed specifically for data analytics. He proposes a four-layer (*http://bit.ly/1G2PcE6*) RTBDA technology stack, shown in Figure 5-1. Although his stack is geared for predictive analytics, it serves as a good general model.

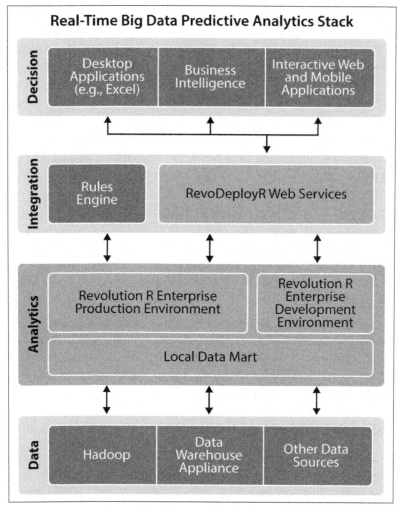

Figure 5-1. From David Smith's presentation, "Real-Time Big Data Analytics: From Deployment to Production" (http://bit.ly/1JpRQE8)

At the foundation is the *data layer*. At this level you have structured data in RDBMS, NoSQL, HBase, or Impala; unstructured data in

Hadoop MapReduce; streaming data from the Web, social media, sensors, and operational systems; and limited capabilities for performing descriptive analytics. Tools such as Hive, HBase, Storm, and Spark also sit at this layer. (Matei Zaharia suggests dividing the data layer into two layers, one for storage and the other for query processing.)

The *analytics layer* sits above the data layer. The analytics layer includes a production environment for deploying real-time scoring and dynamic analytics; a development environment for building models; and a local data mart that is updated periodically from the data layer, situated near the analytics engine to improve performance.

On top of the analytics layer is the *integration layer*. It is the "glue" that holds the end-user applications and analytics engines together, and it usually includes a rules engine or CEP engine, and an API for dynamic analytics that "brokers" communication between app developers and data scientists.

The topmost layer is the *decision layer*. This is where the rubber meets the road, and it can include end-user applications such as desktop, mobile, and interactive web apps, as well as business intelligence software. This is the layer that most people "see." It's the layer at which business analysts, C-suite executives, and customers interact with the real-time big data analytics system.

Again, it's important to note that each layer is associated with different sets of users, and that different sets of users will define "real time" differently. Moreover, the four layers aren't passive lumps of technologies—each layer enables a critical phase of real-time analytics deployment.

The Five Phases of Real Time

Real-time big data analytics is an iterative process involving multiple tools and systems. Smith says that it's helpful to divide the process into five phases: data distillation, model development, validation and deployment, real-time scoring, and model refresh. At each phase, the terms "real time" and "big data" are fluid in meaning. The definitions at each phase of the process are not carved into stone. Indeed, they are context dependent. Like the technology stack discussed earlier, Smith's five-phase process model (*http://bit.ly/*

1JpRQE8) is devised as a framework for predictive analytics. But it also works as a general framework for real-time big data analytics.

1. *Data distillation*—Like unrefined oil, data in the data layer is crude and messy. It lacks the structure required for building models or performing analysis. The data distillation phase includes extracting features for unstructured text, combining disparate data sources, filtering for populations of interest, selecting relevant features and outcomes for modeling, and exporting sets of distilled data to a local data mart (Figure 5-2).

2. *Model development*—Processes in this phase include feature selection, sampling, and aggregation; variable transformation; model estimation; model refinement; and model benchmarking. The goal at this phase is creating a predictive model that is powerful, robust, comprehensible, and implementable. The key requirements for data scientists at this phase are speed, flexibility, productivity, and reproducibility. These requirements are critical in the context of big data: a data scientist will typically construct, refine, and compare dozens of models in the search for a powerful and robust real-time algorithm.

3. *Validation and deployment*—The goal at this phase is testing the model to make sure that it works in the real world. The validation process involves re-extracting fresh data, running it against the model, and comparing results with outcomes run on data that's been withheld as a validation set. If the model works, it can be deployed into a production environment.

4. *Real-time scoring*—In real-time systems, scoring is triggered by actions at the decision layer (by consumers at a website or by an operational system through an API), and the communications are brokered by the integration layer. In the scoring phase, some real-time systems will use the same hardware that's used in the data layer, but they will not use the same data. At this phase of the process, the deployed scoring rules are "divorced" from the data in the data layer or data mart. Note also that at this phase, the limitations of Hadoop become apparent. Hadoop today is not particularly well-suited for real-time scoring, although it can be used for "near real-time" applications such as populating large tables or precomputing scores. Newer technologies, such as Cloudera's Impala, are designed to improve Hadoop's real-time capabilities.

5. *Model refresh*—Data is always changing, so there needs to be a way to refresh the data and refresh the model built on the original data. The existing scripts or programs used to run the data and build the models can be reused to refresh the models. Simple exploratory data analysis is also recommended, along with periodic (weekly, daily, or hourly) model refreshes. The refresh process, as well as validation and deployment, can be automated using web-based services such as RevoDeployR (*http://bit.ly/1NMrSRq*), a part of the Revolution R Enterprise solution.

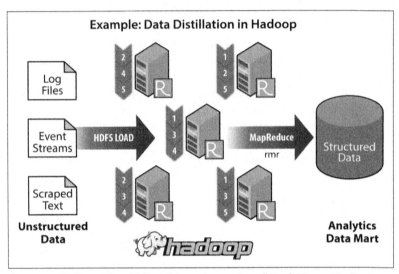

Figure 5-2. From David Smith's presentation, "Real-Time Big Data Analytics: From Deployment to Production" (http://bit.ly/1JpRQE8)

A caveat on the refresh phase: Refreshing the model based on reingesting the data and rerunning the scripts will work for only a limited time, since the underlying data—and even the underlying structure of the data—will eventually change so much that the model will no longer be valid. Important variables can become nonsignificant, nonsignificant variables can become important, and new data sources are continuously emerging. If the model accuracy measure begins drifting, go back to phase 2 and reexamine the data. If necessary, go back to phase 1 and rebuild the model from scratch.

How Big Is Big?

As suggested earlier, the "bigness" of big data depends on its location in the stack. At the data layer, it is not unusual to see petabytes and even exabytes of data. At the analytics layer, you're more likely to encounter gigabytes and terabytes of refined data. By the time you reach the integration layer, you're handling megabytes. At the decision layer, the data sets have dwindled down to kilobytes, and we're measuring data less in terms of scale and more in terms of bandwidth.

The takeaway is that the higher you go in the stack, the less data you need to manage. At the top of the stack, size is considerably less relevant than speed. Now we're talking about real time, and this is where it gets really interesting.

"If you visit the Huffington Post website, for example, you'll see a bunch of ads pop up on the right-hand side of the page," says Smith. "Those ads have been selected for you on the basis of information generated in real time by marketing analytics companies like Upstream Software, which pulls information from a mash-up of multiple sources stored in Hadoop. Those ads have to be selected and displayed within a fraction of a second. Think about how often that's happening. Everybody who's browsing the Web sees hundreds of ads. You're talking about an incredible number of transactions occurring every second."

Part of a Larger Trend

The push toward real-time big data analytics is part of a much larger trend in which the machines we create act less like machines and more like human beings, says Dhiraj Rajaram, founder and CEO of Mu Sigma, a provider of decision sciences and analytics solutions.

"Today, most of our technology infrastructure is not designed for real time," says Rajaram, who worked as a strategy consultant at Booz Allen Hamilton and PricewaterhouseCoopers before launching Mu Sigma. "Our legacy systems are geared for batch processing. We store data in a central location, and when we want a piece of information, we have to find it, retrieve it, and process it. That's the way most systems work. But that isn't the way the human mind works. Human memory is more like flash memory. We have lots of specific knowledge that's already mapped—that's why we can react and respond much more quickly than most of our machines. Our intelligence is distributed, not highly centralized, so more of it resides at the edge. That means we can find it and retrieve it quicker. Real time is a step toward building machines that respond to problems the way people do."

As information technology systems become less monolithic and more distributed, real-time big data analytics will become less exotic and more commonplace. The various technologies of data science will be industrialized, costs will fall, and eventually real-time analytics will become a commodity.

At that point, the focus will shift from data science to the next logical frontier: decision science. "Even if you have the best real-time analytics, you won't be competitive unless you empower the people in the organization to make the right decisions," says Rajaram. "The creation of analytics and the consumption of analytics are two different things. You need processes for translating the analytics into good decisions. Right now, everyone thinks that analytics technology is sexy. But the real challenge isn't transforming the technology —the real challenge is transforming the people and the processes. That's the hard part."

CHAPTER 6

Big Data and the Evolving Role of the CIO

Topline Summary

Fifteen years ago, the primary job of the chief information officer (CIO) was helping the chief financial officer (CFO) reconcile accounts and close the books. On rare occasions, the CIO would interact directly with the chief executive officer (CEO), and on even rarer occasions, the CIO might interact directly with the company's board of directors. The CIO was perceived by senior management as an elevated techie, someone who knew how to fix the printer when it jammed.

The astonishingly rapid growth of consumer technology, e-commerce, social networkings, and cloud technology changed all of that. Today, the CIO has a seat at the table. The modern CIO works alongside other C-level executives, helping the company grow its revenue, delight its customers, develop new products, break into new markets, comply with complex government regulations, *and* keep the printers running.

The rise of big data and advanced analytics makes the CIO's job even more complicated, since many of the legacy systems built and acquired when the CIO was still in high school simply can't handle the volume, velocity, and variety of data generated by the company's operations.

> This report, written in the autumn of 2013, examines how the role
> of the CIO is evolving quickly from an order taker with a fancy
> business title to a business innovator with unprecedented access to
> the highest levels of corporate management.

A Radical Shift in Focus and Perspective

IT traditionally focused on the processes of managing data, rather
than on data itself. The relatively new idea that data itself has intrin-
sic business value is forcing corporate IT departments to rethink
many long-held beliefs about data management. The notion that
data has value—that it is, in fact, the new oil—is having a seismic
impact on the IT function.

"We're going to see a lot of changes in the IT industry," says Harvey
Koeppel, a veteran CIO whose lengthy career includes executive
posts at Citigroup and Chemical Bank, now part of JPMorgan
Chase. "We're at the beginning of an inflection point, and we've
only begun to scratch the surface." Until recently, the primary role
of IT was to enable business processes. From a technology perspective, that role forced IT to focus almost exclusively on the programs
running underneath those business processes.

"That master/slave relationship is drawing to an end," says Koeppel.
The reason for the sea change seems relatively simple on its surface:
many companies now perceive that their data has more inherent
business value than all the various processes and technologies necessary for managing that data.

"Historically, the IT industry was based on a process paradigm,"
says Fred Balboni, who leads the big data and analytics practice in
IBM Global Business Services. "You kept your eyes on the process.
You were more interested in the pipeline than in what the pipeline
was carrying."

If data truly is the new oil, then what is the proper role of IT in a
global economy that is fueled by data? Is IT analogous to the oil
industry's drilling equipment, pipelines, refineries, and gas stations?
Or does IT have a strategic role to play in the age of big data? And if
IT does indeed have a strategic role, what is the proper role of the
CIO?

"IT has focused traditionally on building reports about events that happened in the past. Big data is now shifting the focus of IT. Instead of just looking backward, IT can develop the capabilities for looking forward," says Clifton Triplett, a West Point graduate who has held senior executive IT posts at Baker Hughes, Motorola, General Motors, Allied Signal, and Entergy Services. "Going forward, IT will be far more instrumental in predicting future opportunities and strategies based on statistical information. As a result, IT will become much more important." Shifting from a backward-looking to a more forward-looking role will require IT to change its view of data. "IT will have to understand data in a business context," says Triplett. "IT will have to acquire new skills for managing and understanding data. Today, the average IT person doesn't have those skills."

In other words, IT must learn to perceive data in a way that's similar to the way that the business perceives data. As IT develops more expertise and a deeper understanding of big data analytic techniques, "You will begin to see a stronger integration of IT and the business," says Triplett.

Ashish Sinha, who leads the Data Warehouse Technologies group at MasterCard, agrees that IT is poised for a significant transformation. In its earliest days, IT was known as management information systems (MIS). Over time, MIS has evolved from a purely reporting function into a fully fledged corporate department that oversees virtually every business process occurring within the modern enterprise.

Despite its enhanced scope and larger budget, IT still exerts relatively little influence on the development of business strategy. Thanks to big data, however, that "influence gap" is on the verge of vanishing. "Big data technology allows companies to harness the power of predictive analytics, extract value from their data, and monetize it," says Sinha. For the first time in its history, IT has the potential to transform itself from a cost center into a profit center. For the CIO, the upside is clear: when you lead a department that makes money for the company, you get a seat at the table when strategy is discussed. If you are the CIO, big data is your new best friend.

Getting from Here to There

Leveraging big data analytics to transform the IT department from a cost center to a profit center will require new skills and capabilities. From Sinha's perspective, IT departments should focus on developing or acquiring the following:

- Data cataloging and storage techniques that allow easy access to data by analysts
- Big data appliances, databases, data access, and data visualization tools
- Capabilities for tapping external data sources
- Information security awareness and process expertise required for designing data access procedures that comply with the company's data privacy policies

"CIOs have to realize that they are responsible for protecting and managing an extremely valuable asset that if used properly can become a huge competitive advantage, and if used improperly can lead to a disaster," says Sinha.

The good news is that many of the skills and capabilities required for managing big data initiatives can be taught to existing staff, acquired by hiring people with analytic training, or "rented" from a rapidly expanding universe of consulting firms specializing in big data. And here's more good news: getting up to speed on big data does not necessarily require the wholesale abandonment of legacy IT infrastructure. For example, you will not have to decommission your existing data warehouse.

"Some fundamental beliefs around data warehouses will have to change," says Sinha. "The traditional model requires data in the warehouse to be 'clean' and 'structured.' We have to get comfortable with the idea that data can—and will—be 'messy' and 'unstructured,' and that we will have to use external data sources (which have traditionally not been pulled into enterprise data warehouses) in new and innovative ways that will translate the cacophony into a symphony."

Behind and Beyond the Application

Eben Hewitt is the chief technology officer at Choice Hotels International and the author of *Cassandra: The Definitive Guide* (O'Reilly). He believes that big data is driving a major change in the way that business users perceive IT. "In the past, the business saw traditional IT as the infrastructure group, the database administrators, and the application developers. Most users defined IT as the applications on their desktop, which makes sense because those applications are the user interface," says Hewitt. "But the applications are only the window dressing around the data, and people tend to focus on details like whether the little button on the application is green or blue."

The reality is that most people don't really care about the applications. They care about their year-over-year sales numbers, how many prospects they have in the sales pipeline, how much revenue they're generating—information that's directly related to their job performance and their earnings. The arrival of big data, with its implicit promise to reveal useful details about customers and their buying behavior, suddenly makes IT a lot more interesting to many more people than it ever was before.

"Big data makes IT much more visible and much more interesting to the average user," says Hewitt. "Now the conversation isn't about the application and whether the little button is green or blue—the conversation is about the data. Now IT and the business are speaking the same language. The users are much more comfortable talking about data than they are talking about applications, and so they are more willing to talk to IT and engage in meaningful conversations."

The consumerization of IT—which is shorthand for saying that everyone with a mobile phone or a tablet has become a programmer to one degree or another—has created a new class of empowered and sophisticated IT users. "There is no such thing as a business user who knows nothing about technology. That person no longer exists," says Hewitt. "As a result, the conversations between the business and IT have become much more sophisticated and more technical. The business users ask us about the scalability of our servers. They ask us about web log data. They want to know how the data is aggregated. Those are conversations that wouldn't have happened before big data."

Whether you think that higher levels of user sophistication are a good thing or a bad thing is largely irrelevant. Today's users have a better grasp of technology and zero tolerance for applications that don't work or can't deliver meaningful results. That's the new normal, and woe betide the IT executive who doesn't see that the game has changed.

"You need to start preparing now or you'll be playing catch-up," says Jonathan Reichental, the CIO of the City of Palo Alto. "The role of IT is changing fast in many positive ways. We're not just the guys who buy servers and put them in racks. We're adding new value by helping the C-suite and the line of service leaders see the invisible, to find hidden patterns and to make better decisions."

Department directors increasingly rely on IT to provide information that enables them to improve services, increase efficiency, and manage costs. "This is a whole new role for the CIO. In the past, our job was deploying systems, doing the heavy lifting. Now it's more about making sure that people have the data they need to do their jobs better," says Reichental.

That's not to suggest that IT infrastructure is going away anytime soon. Even if it moves off-premise, it still exists somewhere, and that means that the CIO will be responsible for making sure it's delivering value to the business. Storage and tools aren't likely to pose major headaches for the CIO, but understanding how all the various parts of the emerging big data infrastructure relate to one another will be important. Below is a simplified diagram of a generic big data analytics stack:[1]

---

1 A more detailed version of this diagram, originally proposed by David Smith of Revolution Analytics, can be found in Chapter 5. The descriptions of each layer originally appeared in that paper.

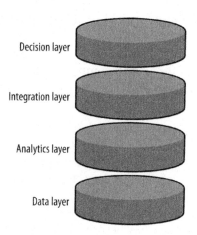

Decision layer

Integration layer

Analytics layer

Data layer

Investing in Big Data Infrastructure

One of the major attractions of Hadoop is that it's an open source platform that runs on relatively inexpensive commodity hardware. That being said, no one is seriously suggesting that the costs of implementing big data solutions are trivial.

While it is true that many big data implementations do not require huge capital investments on the scale required for, say, buying a new ERP system or building a global e-commerce platform, developing the capabilities required for managing big data regularly on a commercial basis isn't cheap. Companies such as Google, Facebook, Amazon, and Yahoo! have spent hundreds of millions of dollars building big data systems.

"The investment required for handling big data can be massive," says José Carlos Eiras, the former CIO of General Motors Europe and the author of *The Practical CIO* (*http://amzn.to/1MECxPf*) (Wiley). Eiras quickly dispels the myth that big data operations can be simply "outsourced to the cloud," noting that in Europe and other parts of the world, the use and movement of data is strictly regulated.

The existence of strong regulatory controls, along with growing concern about the potential misuse of big data, means that IT departments will be spending more time and more resources making sure that data is stored safely and securely. Eiras believes that big data will force IT to revert back to its original role of "guardian of all data," a role that it had largely abandoned after the rise of e-commerce in the late 1990s and first decade of the 21st century. "For the past 20 years, IT has tried to make the business units and the business users responsible for data," says Eiras. "But a change is already occurring, especially in companies where big data is a source of big money. The responsibility for managing data is shifting back to the IT function."

That doesn't mean that CIOs will abandon their efforts to push non-essential IT operations into the cloud. It does mean, however, that the cloud is not some kind of quasi-magical, one-size-fits-all low-cost panacea for resolving big data challenges. In many respects, it makes sense for IT to reclaim its birthright as the primary manager of corporate data. Another and perhaps less kind way of saying it would be that big data has become too important to leave to the amateurs.

Even if that sounds harsh, it's worth remembering that the job of the business user is achieving a specific business result, and not worrying about the underlying technologies that make it all possible. Ideally, all of the various components and systems work together seamlessly to produce a desired result and should be largely invisible to the business user.

Providing seamless integration and interoperability of multiple tools and systems is clearly the domain of IT. "There is no single architecture that fits everything together," says David Champagne, chief architect at Revolution Analytics. "You're going to need a collection of analytics systems and an understanding of how all the various pieces work together. It's not a black-and-white situation." Champagne envisions hybrid architectures of multiple systems running in concert to generate results for users seeking specific types of information. "Not every piece of data is interesting. A lot of it is noise. You will have to figure out what kind of data you have and the kind of analytics you need to run," he says.

The answers to those types of critical questions will provide the outline of the technology architecture required to handle your big data. It would be unwise, says Champagne, for organizations to skip ahead without answering the critical questions first. "The myth about big data is that you have to use all of it," he says. "If your problem doesn't require all the data, why use it?"

Determining which elements of your data sets are genuinely necessary for answering your questions will guide you toward making the right infrastructure investments. Again, this seems to be a task that is best handled by IT. CIOs are accustomed to wading through tidal waves of conflicting requests from business units. And CIOs know better than to blindly trust vendors promising all-encompassing solutions.

Does the CIO Still Matter?

Mike Flowers is a rock star in the world of big data. As chief analytics officer for the City of New York, Flowers has won praise for using big data to track down polluters, identify unsafe housing, speed up permit processing, and generally improve the quality of life in the Big Apple. He attributes part of his success to the team of energetic young data scientists he has assembled and part to his close working relationship with the city's CIO, Rahul Merchant. "I don't make the infrastructure decisions," says Flowers. "I explain what I need to deliver insights for improving operations, and Rahul provides the technology. It's really a seamless conversation between operations, analytics, and IT. We're all working together toward a common goal of providing better service across the city."

The key to the city's successful use of big data is that "seamless conversation" between critical stakeholders. Take one of them out of the loop, and the model falls apart. "Rahul is very smart and he spent a lot of time in the business sector. He knows that IT can't deliver value without input from the key players. I would say that big data is definitely a team sport and that IT is absolutely essential," says Flowers.

From Capex to Opex

Several of the IT executives interviewed for this white paper also suggested that a series of big data initiatives (which would necessarily include new investments in people, processes, and technology) would accelerate the transformation of IT from a slow-moving culture focused on managing its capital expenses (capex) to a more nimble culture focused on managing its operating expenses (opex).

That shift from a capex mentality to an opex mentality might not seem like a big deal. But in addition to forcing a dramatic change from past practices, it would position IT for a more prominent and substantive role in the formulation and execution of corporate strategy. It would also tend to slow the growth of so-called "shadow IT," a relatively common phenomenon in which business units within the company lose patience with the CIO and begin making deals directly with IT suppliers. Because CIOs have traditionally focused on capex, which tends to be less flexible than opex, CIOs are perceived, rightly or wrongly, as being slow to capitalize on new technologies that would provide the company's business units with advantages over the competitors in highly time-sensitive markets.

Gregory Fell, the former CIO of Terex Corp. and the author of *Decoding the IT Value Problem* (*http://amzn.to/1LInnCX*) (Wiley) puts it succinctly: "For quite a while, IT has been called 'the office of no.' Smart CIOs work hard at transforming IT into 'the office of know.' When you're leading 'the office of know,' people come to you for help, instead of going around you." Fell suggests that CIOs focus on understanding the real business value of big data solutions. "Big data enables us to answer questions that we couldn't answer before," says Fell, currently the chief strategy officer at Crisply, a data services company. "But first we need to know how much money it costs to answer those questions."

In the past, there were many questions that IT simply could not answer. "In the age of big data, the challenge is doing the cost-benefit analysis," says Fell. "In other words, how much are you willing to spend to know the answer to your question?" Fell's point is well taken, and it points to a maturation of the CIO's role as a sort of corporate consigliere—someone who is trusted implicitly at the highest levels of the organization.

In any event, a significant expansion in the strategic role of IT would elevate the status of the CIO and would greatly enhance the bargaining power of IT during budget negotiations. So from the perspective of IT, big data would launch a virtuous circle of self-reinforcing benefits.

A More Nimble Mindset

Some experienced IT practitioners see today's "big data versus traditional data" narrative as a variation on the "Agile" versus "Waterfall" software development narratives from the previous decade. The comparison has some validity, and it's helpful to look at the similarities between Agile methods and big data.

Both Agile and big data reflect more of a user- or customer-centric view of the world than their decidedly product- or process-centric predecessors. Agile and big data both tend to push people out of their natural comfort zones and require higher levels of tolerance for ambiguity and uncertainty. Both, one could argue, are messier and less formally structured than what came before them. "IT people who are comfortable working in an Agile environment are likely to be more comfortable working with big data than people who worked with a traditional software development life cycle (SDLC) model," says Jim Tosone, a former director of the Healthcare Informatics Group at Pfizer Pharmaceuticals. "Agile is about simplicity, speed, and pragmatism. With Agile, you learn to work with what you've got."

Tosone recommends staffing big data initiatives with people who enjoy exploring problems and who don't feel the need for immediate closure. "A lot of IT people have a very strong desire to find a solution very quickly and then move on to the next problem," says Tosone. "But their need for closure cuts them off from the kinds of exploration that are often necessary for achieving true understanding of problems."

Tosone is now a management coach and uses techniques that he learned when he joined an improvisation group earlier in his career at Pfizer. He is also an accomplished classical guitarist, and he sees a distinct connection between music, improv, and big data analytics. "With big data, it's unlikely that you're going to know exactly what you need up front," says Tosone. "So you have to build flexible models and flexible tools. Working with big data requires right-brain and left-brain thinking. You need your whole brain working on the problem. The ideal data scientist is part mathematician and part musician."

While that idealized description does not match most of today's IT workforce, it would be a good model to keep in mind when hiring the next generation of IT employees. And even if you are not a strong proponent of Agile methodology, the important message is that IT organizations need to become more nimble, more flexible, and more open to change in the age of big data.

Looking to the Future

It appears certain that big data and its associated technologies are destined to become an essential part of the CIO's portfolio. Sooner or later, all new technologies fall under the purview of IT, and it seems unlikely that big data will be the exception. In the long term, it's a sure bet that big data will evolve into a multidisciplinary practice, spread across various functional units of the enterprise. It's entirely plausible that big data will become a standard element of integrated customer strategy and will disappear as a separate or specialized process.

Gary Reiner, the former CIO of General Electric and an operating partner at General Atlantic, foresees a close working relationship between the CIO and a newer type of executive, the chief analytics officer (CAO). "There will be a partnership between the CIO and the CAO. Or in some instances, the CIO will also act as the CAO. It will depend on the needs of the company and on the personality of the CIO," says Reiner. "The point is that big data is an interdisciplinary effort. I'm a huge believer in cross-functional decision making and cross-functional collaboration. When single functions take sole responsibility for important projects, they are rarely successful. Everyone has to work together."

At the most fundamental level, big data is likely to create greater demand for IT people who are familiar with data analytics. Demand for skills related to server management and network administration is likely to decline. The need for traditional IT skills won't vanish entirely, but they will recede in significance as big data moves into the foreground.

While it's difficult to predict exactly which skills will be in demand two or three years from now, it seems reasonably certain that companies will be looking for people who understand data, understand business, and can write software code.

"If I could say what the next big skill to have is, I'd be taking a class in it right now," says Sarah Henochowicz, manager of business intelligence at Tumblr. "In my role, knowing SQL and Python are the most valuable skills. I use R a little bit. Honestly, when it gets down to what language you're programming in, I think that being able to understand the logic is the most important piece. Not necessarily knowing the syntax, but knowing the structure behind it.

Once you know a programming language, it's not that difficult switching to another language. A lot of programs can do the same things, and there are tons of resources online that can help you figure them out. But understanding the logic is what's really important."

Now Is the Time to Prepare

As new technologies emerge, the role of the CIO changes. An ongoing challenge for all CIOs is to figure out which new technologies require immediate responses and which can wait. Most CIOs are still in the process of developing strategies for cloud, mobile, and social computing. Security and regulatory compliance are major headaches. Many CIOs spend a significant portion of their time managing a wide range of IT service vendors and outsourcers. CIOs are under pressure to continue cutting costs while adding new services and retraining IT staffers to become more "customer centric." For most CIOs, big data has not yet risen to the level of an immediate crisis.

That perception could easily change, just as perceptions about the value of e-commerce changed rapidly following the successes of companies such as Amazon and eBay. There is no reason to assume that big data won't be the "next big thing."

In any event, CIOs are likely to be questioned by their C-level colleagues about big data, so it makes sense to be prepared. At minimum, CIOs should read about big data, attend conferences, and listen to sales presentations from big data vendors. Smart CIOs will begin hiring deputies who understand the various ways in which big data can help the business. Ideally, CIOs will encourage the hiring of IT staffers who understand database technology, have relevant business experience, and are comfortable writing code.

It seems certain that big data will have its day. For CIOs, the big question is, "Will we be ready when that day arrives?"

CHAPTER 7

Building Functional Teams for the IoT Economy

Topline Summary

Developing products and services for the Internet of Things will require levels of collaboration and information sharing that might seem extreme or even risky when compared to conventional standards. As digital on-demand manufacturing becomes the norm rather than the exception, however, the traditional linear process of software developers throwing code "over the wall" to hardware designers who then throw their designs "over the wall" to manufacturers is clearly obsolete. If the IoT is going to work, all of the relationships across the extended value chain will need to be reevaluated, rethought, and realigned.

This report, written in 2015 for the O'Reilly Solid Conference in San Francisco, describes the challenges of building functional teams of software developers, hardware designers, and manufacturers for the emerging IoT economy.

You don't have to be a hardcore dystopian to imagine the problems that can unfold when worlds of software collide with worlds of hardware.

When you consider the emerging economics of the Internet of Things (IoT), the challenges grow exponentially, and the complexities are daunting.

For many people, the IoT suggests a marriage of software and hardware. But the economics of the IoT involves more than a simple binary coupling. In addition to software development and hardware design, a viable end-to-end IoT process would include prototyping, sourcing raw materials, manufacturing, operations, marketing, sales, distribution, customer support, finance, legal, and HR.

It's reasonable to assume that an IoT process would be part of a larger commercial business strategy that also involves multiple sales and distribution channels (for example, wholesale, retail, value-added reseller, direct), warehousing, operations, and interactions with a host of regulatory agencies at various levels of government, depending on the city, state, region, and country.

A diagram of a truly functional IoT would look less like a traditional linear supply chain and more like an ecosystem or a network. The most basic supply chain looks something like this:

```
Supplier → Producer → Consumer
```

If we took a similarly linear approach and mapped it to a hypothetical IoT scenario, it might look something like this:

```
Entrepreneurs → Capital Markets and Investors → Sales →
Software Development → Hardware Design → Prototyping →
Manufacture → Warehousing → Distribution/Logistics →
Wholesale → Retail → Consumer Markets → Customer Service →
Finance → Legal → HR → Regulators
```

Even an abbreviated description of a hypothetical IoT "supply chain" reveals the futility of attempting to map a simple linear sequential model onto a multidimensional framework of interconnected high-velocity processes requiring near-real-time feedback. A practical IoT ecosystem model would look something like Figure 7-1.

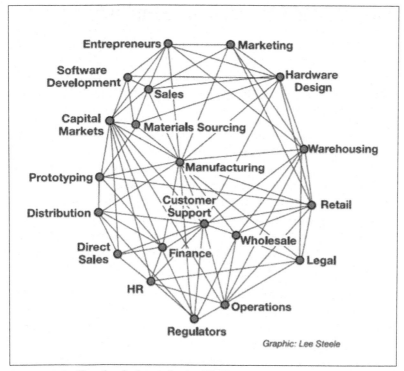

Figure 7-1. Sketch of a hypothetical IoT ecosystem

In all likelihood, the IoT economy will resemble a network of inter-related functions, responsibilities, and stakeholders. The sketch gives only a rough idea of the complexities involved—each node would have its own galaxy of interconnected processes, technologies, organizations, and stakeholders. In any case, it's a far cry from simple "upstream/downstream" charts that make supply chains seem like smoothly flowing rivers of pure commercial activity.

Unlike traditional software development scenarios, IoT projects are undertaken with the "real world" clearly in mind. It's understood that IoT services and products will "touch" the physical universe we live in. If the assignment is developing new parts for jet engines used by passenger airlines, real consequences will arise if the parts don't work as promised.

A More Fluid Approach to Team Building

Working relationships between software developers, hardware designers, and manufacturers within IoT ecosystems are still taking shape and evolving. The structure, staffing, and organization of a team would depend largely on the project at hand and the depth of available talent.

"There isn't an ideal team. You have to start with the problem and work backwards to discover what is available and commoditized, and what really needs to be created to make a solution real," says Andrew Clay Shafer, senior director of technology at Pivotal (*http://pivotal.io/*), a company that provides a cloud platform for IoT developers. "The dream team would have unlimited resources, expertise, and imagination. Realistically, you won't have a dream team, so you are better off examining the problem, looking at your available resources, and filling in gaps."

Mike Estee, CTO and cofounder of Other Machine Co. (*https://othermachine.co/*) , a company that builds machines and creates software for desktop manufacturing, says the firm looks for software developers with experience in "building consumer-facing applications that integrate directly with hardware designed in tandem," and hardware designers who can bring products to market "on time, on budget, and with a high degree of polish."

Ayah Bdeir is the founder and CEO of littleBits (*http://littlebits.cc/*), a company that creates "libraries" of electronic modules that snap together with magnets. An advocate of the open source hardware movement, she is a cofounder of the Open Hardware Summit (*http://2013.oshwa.org/about/*), a TED Senior Fellow (*http://www.ted.com/people/fellows*), and an alumna of the MIT Media Lab (*http://bit.ly/1QZSPkF*). From her perspective, the "ideal" development team includes hardware, firmware, software, and web experts. Tightly integrating the design function is absolutely critical, she says.

"Design is crucial at the very beginning. Our second hire in the company was an industrial designer, and it has transformed our business and our product," Bdeir says. "Specific skills and languages don't always mean as much as the ability to adapt. The team needs to be creative, agile, and quick to learn."

While software development is considered a relatively "mature" field, the need to combine software development and hardware design has spawned a host of new problems. In an email, Bdeir shared her view of the current situation:

> For software developers, a lot of the barriers have been removed. Today, you can prototype and launch a software product with very little time, money, and most importantly, few external dependencies. When you see there is traction, you can scale your offering gradually, and not overextend yourself financially.
>
> For hardware, the barriers are much more defined and difficult to deal with. You can prototype a lot faster, and get initial interest/traction through Kickstarter, press, or showing off your product at events. But there is a pretty big step to getting first-run manufacturing done.
>
> Finding manufacturing partners who will help you make your product manufacturable is hard when you are at a small scale, and it takes a lot of time. When we were starting out, we had to manufacture our magnetic connector with a factory that made plastic insoles and knee guards because I couldn't find any manufacturer that knew electronics or connectors that would take me seriously.

Estee, who spent nine years as a software engineer at Apple, has a similarly chastened view of the challenges. Here's a brief excerpt from an essay (*http://bit.ly/1V9u2R1*) he posted recently on Medium:

> If you've never started a hardware company before, it's very hard to understand the vast differences between a prototype, a product, and a company which supports it. A product is so much more than just the machine. It's also the packaging, the quality assurance plan, documentation, the factory, the supply chain, vendor relations, testing, certification, distribution, sales, accounting, human resources, and a health plan. It goes on and on. All things you probably weren't thinking about in the rush to get the Kickstarter launched.

Indeed, the complexities seem nearly inexhaustible. Shafer describes the challenges from an industry-wide perspective:

> As we move into a world where all things are integrated, the stack is getting wider and deeper. The choice is between building teams that have expertise at each level...or choosing platforms to do the heavy lifting and act as force multipliers for teams with more focused skills. The challenge is deciding which problems to solve yourself and which to outsource.
>
> People get excited about creating "things," but the Internet is the other half of the equation, and there are still hard problems to solve

there. Even moderate IoT build-outs could quickly create sensor networks that have latency, scaling, and analytics problems that only a handful of the big web companies have had to solve until now.

Today, there is no equivalent to the LAMP[1] stack for the IoT. It will be several years before a common way of solving IoT problems begins to emerge.

Raising the Bar on Collaboration

At least one evolutionary path seems fairly certain: developing products and services for the IoT will require significantly higher levels of collaboration and information sharing than those considered normal or acceptable in traditional development scenarios.

Harel Kodesh, vice president and CTO at GE Software, recalls when software development was a mostly solitary endeavor. "Now it's a team sport to the extreme," he says. "We have many more releases, but the prototypes are smaller, and there are many more components. When I was at Microsoft in 1998, you sat at your workstation and the only thing you had to think about was the code you were writing. At the end of the day, or the end of the week, someone called the 'build master' would go around, collect the code everyone had written, compile it, and try to get it to work."

Since testing was only partially automated, most of it was done manually. It wasn't unusual for a company to spend five years developing and testing code for a new operating system. Today, development and testing move at greatly accelerated speeds. People generally expect software and related systems to work—especially when they're developed for the IoT.

The biggest difference between then and now, Kodesh says, is the cloud. In the past, developers ran code on workstations; now they run it in the cloud. For IoT development teams, the cloud is a blessing and a curse. The cloud's ability to deliver scale at a moment's notice makes it invaluable and indispensable for developing IoT products and services. GE believes in its cloud development model. But if you're a passenger riding in a high-speed train that's built

---

1 LAMP stands for Linux, Apache, MySQL, and PHP.

with subcomponents that were designed in the cloud, should you be concerned?

Those kinds of concerns are leading GE and other organizations, such as National Aeronautics and Space Administration (NASA) (*http://www.nasa.gov/*) and the US Air Force, to explore the creation of "digital twins," which are extremely accurate software abstractions of complicated physical objects and systems. A digital twin would be linked to its physical counterpart through the IoT. The steady flow of data from the real world means the digital twin can be updated continuously, enabling it to "mirror" the conditions of its physical counterpart in real time.

Ideally, digital twins would serve as "living" models for machines and systems in physical space. And since it's unlikely that software developers would have access to jet engines or diesel locomotives while they're in service, the digital twin concept is expected to play a major role in the evolution of IoT development and design processes. In case you don't believe the IoT will have any impact on you personally, doctors are already talking about using digital twins in healthcare scenarios. A recent article in The Guardian (*http://bit.ly/1Mq2q2v*) mentions the possibility of creating digital twins for soldiers before they deploy for combat missions, which would allow doctors to create replacement parts for wounded soldiers quickly and accurately.

Worlds Within Worlds

Looking under the hood of an IoT software development process reveals even more complexity. IoT applications are often built from communities of smaller independent processes called *microservices*. Facebook and Google are common examples of microservices architecture. Users are typically unaware of the granularity of the application until a particular component, such as your newsfeed on Facebook, stops working. Usually the glitch sorts itself out quickly, and you don't even realize that part of the application had crashed.

Microservices architecture is particularly useful in IoT scenarios because it enables developers to create highly usable applications that are extremely scalable and easy to replace. In a sense, microservices architecture is reminiscent of service-oriented architecture (SOA), except that SOA was conceived to integrate multiple applications using a service bus architecture; with microservices, however, the service endpoints interact with each other directly to deliver a user-level application.

In his role as head of software engineering for Predix at GE Software, Hima Mukkamala supervises teams of developers working to create the microservices required for real-world IoT applications. In one situation, an oil production operator needed to compare the output of two production lines. "They asked us to build an asset performance management (APM) application so they could compare the two production lines and determine what changes were necessary so the two lines would produce the same amounts of oil," Mukkamala explains.

Traditional development techniques would have taken months to produce a useful set of software tools for the business problem. Normally, that type of project would have involved separate teams for software development, hardware design, testing, monitoring, and deployment. Using a DevOps-style approach cut the time required from six months to six weeks.

Mukkamala says he was surprised by the relative ease of coding, building, monitoring, and deploying viable applications created from microservices. "I thought that would be harder, but it was less of a challenge than I had imagined," he recalls. "What I thought would be easy, however, was transitioning from a traditional software development model to a DevOps model. That turned out to be a much more stressful challenge. For developers accustomed to a traditional SRA (software requirements analysis) approach, writing and deploying code every day was a shock."

As CIOs like to say, "It's never just technology. It's always people, process, and technology." Mukkamala's hands-on experience testifies to the importance of acknowledging cultural barriers and implementing a change management process.

"In times past, developers would write code and throw it over the wall. Now they have to work very closely with the operations people," he says. "Collaboration between developers and ops people has to start from day one. Developers have to think like people in ops, and people in ops have to think like developers. Now we act like one team, all the way from development to operations."

Vineet Banga is a development manager at GE Software. Working with Kodesh and Mukkamala, he often serves as a "human bridge" connecting senior management, software development, operations, and "machine teams" that finalize the marriage of code and physical devices.

"We're moving out of our normal comfort zones and constantly trying to broaden our horizons," he says. "The result is that our efforts are now always overlapping, which is good. On the development side, we're looking more at hardware/operations and on the operations side, they're looking more at software."

Teams that were highly specialized a few years ago are now much more cross-functional and multidisciplinary. Team members are expected to write code in a variety of programming languages and be comfortable working with different layers of the software stack

A typical team might consist of two Java engineers, a web UI developer, a security engineer, and two engineers with hands-on infrastructure experience. Depending on the project, a team might include a Java developer, a software architect, a Linux systems developer, and user experience developer.

In any event, the team would be responsible for making sure the code they write provides the levels of scale, security, interoperability, and compliance required for the project. "We try to delegate as many decisions as possible to the team," Banga says. "When you have six or seven people from different backgrounds working together, sometimes the best decisions are made by the team itself, and not by managers or executives."

Supply Chain to Mars

Michael Galluzzi is lead business strategist for additive manufacturing and supply chain management at the NASA Swamp Works Lab at Kennedy Space Center, Florida. From his perspective, the challenges of creating an IoT economy aren't confined to Earth—they extend into deep space.

Imagine this scenario: NASA sends a spacecraft to Mars. Everything goes fine. Ten years after the spacecraft lands, its rover transmits an alert indicating the imminent failure of a critical part.

In a perfect imaginary world based on traditional logistics and current technologies, a spare part for the rover would be sitting in a warehouse somewhere and would be dispatched to Mars on the next available rocket. The reality is far more complicated.

Aside from the fact that we don't send rockets to Mars on a regular schedule, not to mention the time it takes to get there, it's unlikely in these days of just-in-time (JIT) manufacturing that a backup version of the part would be available from Earth-based sources. A new part would need to be manufactured using *in situ* resources or ideally using regolith-based 3D printing or additive manufacturing technology, which NASA Swamp Works Lab is currently developing.

But here's where it gets really tricky: spacecraft parts are built to rigid specifications. Companies that produce spacecraft parts are carefully vetted by the government and its various regulatory agencies. Those kinds of companies tend to be small, and they often go out of business. So there's a very strong likelihood that the company that made the original part no longer exists—it's simple macroeconomics (that is, low or no demand, no supply). That raises more problems: Who owns the IP for the part? Who has the expertise and experience required to manufacture the part to NASA's specifications?

If the part is manufactured from rare earth minerals (and many spacecraft parts are indeed made from exotic raw materials), are those minerals still available, and what kinds of permissions will be required to obtain them?

Ideally, an IoT economy would be capable of solving those kinds of problems. But the IoT still lacks critical chunks of infrastructure, such as a common data platform with neural networking capabilities for sharing information up and down the value chain. In addition to data integration challenges, there are data-quality issues. Some suppliers have invested in bleeding-edge advanced analytics, but many others still rely on Excel.

NASA typically deals with thousands of suppliers, from very large to small—high-tech "mom and pop" firms that produce small batches of highly specialized parts—and there's no common data ontology or digital thread for sharing the kinds of highly detailed data required for creating replacement parts and sending them to other planets.

"The supplier community can't access the data they need because the legacy information systems are not connected," Galluzzi says. "The challenge is integrating the information systems down to suppliers at the lowest tiers of the supply chain to obtain the supply chain visibility needed to understand the multifunctional relationships of suppliers or, at minimum, to mitigate counterfeit parts or supply chain disruption."

The future, he says, will be written by organizations that develop capabilities for sourcing and distributing relevant data content at every link and life cycle of the value chain, from development of new products and services to delivery—even when the consumers are located on Mars.

Rethinking Manufacturing from the Ground Up

Even if your supply chain doesn't extend to Mars or beyond, the IoT is forcing suppliers at all levels to rethink and reenvision the standard manufacturing models that have long served the world's industrial societies.

"The supply chain is an old term that conjures up processes that are linked together at every step, when in fact, they are diversified networks of suppliers," says Dennis Thompson, who leads the manufacturing and supply chain services group at SCRA (*http://scra.org/*), an applied research company working with federal and corporate clients. He also serves in leadership roles at two public-private partnerships, the Digital Manufacturing and Design Innovation Institute (DMDII) (*http://dmdii.uilabs.org/*) and the National Digital Engineering and Manufacturing Consortium (NDEMC) (*http://ndemc.org/*).

Henry Ford's idea of supply chain management, for example, was a vertically integrated corporation that owned or operated suppliers at every level of the production process, from hauling iron ore to delivering finished automobiles to a dealer's showroom. "Today, we need to find ways of creating networks of suppliers and managing them as if they were vertically integrated, without owning their assets," Thompson says.

At the DMDII, efforts are underway to invent a new generation of flexible supplier networks. "The challenge is pulling together networks of suppliers around projects, and then disassembling those networks when the projects are finished and new projects come up," Thompson says. One of the tools necessary for creating agile supplier networks is "a next-generation ERP system that would link suppliers on a common platform."

DDMII is building an open source software platform called the Digital Manufacturing Commons (DMC) for suppliers in the digital manufacturing economy. Some have already described the DMC as an industrial version of SimCity, while others see it as a virtual hub enabling communities of developers and suppliers to share information more effectively. Thompson is optimistic the DMC project will bear fruit, and so are DDMII's corporate backers, which include companies such as Boeing, Lockheed Martin, Rolls-Royce, GE, Microsoft, Siemens, and Caterpillar. "They're anticipating getting a return on their investment," Thompson says.

Viva la Revolución?

Technology revolutions are typically accompanied or followed by cultural revolutions, and the IoT revolution is unlikely to break the pattern. As suggested earlier in this report, the primary challenges facing IoT pioneers aren't technical. The hard parts of the problem involve getting disparate players such as software developers, hardware designers, and mechanical engineers to share knowledge and work collaboratively toward achieving common goals. It seems likely that new forms of management will be required, as well as new approaches to concepts such as intellectual property and corporate secrecy.

"I think it comes back to getting the right people at the table and pulling together networks of designers, developers, manufacturers, and sales people," says Thompson. "The voice of the customer should be represented. If you build it, will they buy it? That's a question you've got to ask."

As product development cycles become shorter, incorporating the "voice of the customer" might become less of an afterthought and more of a standard checklist item.

The idea of "failing fast" has also gained traction in digital manufacturing circles. "Agile manufacturing is possible," says Shashank Samala, cofounder of Tempo Automation (*http://tempoautoma*

tion.com/), whose specialty is automating the manufacture of electronics. "Agile is relative, not absolute. If we can make manufacturing 10 times more agile than it is today, that will be an achievement."

It's easy for software developers to be "agile" because there are already huge libraries of code to draw from, and developers rarely have to start from scratch. "With software, you can turn your ideas into actual products very quickly. Most of the knowledge has already been abstracted. It's more difficult to create new hardware quickly, because we don't have modules that we can build on," says Samala. "That's why hardware is harder to develop than software. But we are moving in the right direction."

Still, it seems as though software development races along while hardware development moves at a glacial pace. Bdeir sees the apparent dichotomy as less of a problem and more of a potential business opportunity for companies such as littleBits:

> Making a good product always takes time, whether it's hardware or software. The difference is that with hardware, it either works or it doesn't. You can't iterate when something is on the market. So your MVP (minimum viable product) barrier has to be a lot higher.
>
> We have a ways to go to raise the bar of development in hardware. Every hardware developer is practically starting from scratch: figuring out power distribution, sensor conditioning, getting drivers of hardware to talk to each other. It's the equivalent of coding in assembly. We can and should simplify hardware design by making the design process more open and more accessible and most importantly, more modular so you can raise the level of abstraction from the component level to the interaction level. That has been the guiding principle behind littleBits: stop wasting your time figuring out what the right resistor for that motor is, and focus on the motion that you need to make a magical experience.

CHAPTER 8

Predictive Maintenance: A World of Zero Unplanned Downtime

For want of a nail, the shoe was lost.
For want of a shoe, the horse was lost.
For want of a horse, the rider was lost.
For want of a rider, the message was lost.
For want of a message, the battle was lost.
For want of a battle, the kingdom was lost.
And all for the want of a horseshoe nail.

—Traditional rhyme

Topline Summary

In the old days, the only real way to measure the life span of a machine was running it until it broke. The problem with that approach is that you can never be quite sure when a machine will break. If it breaks on a Sunday morning, when nobody desperately needs whatever the machine does, then it's not a big deal. But if it breaks on a busy day, during peak business hours, then you're looking at problems. If the machine in question is a jet engine on an airliner crossing the Pacific, you're looking at really serious problems.

Now imagine a world in which machines and systems never break down unexpectedly. That's the goal of predictive maintenance: no surprises. Predictive maintenance requires a combination of sensor-equipped machines, networks, and advanced analytics. This report, written in January 2015, examines the emerging field of pre-

> dictive maintenance and describes its role in our increasingly automated societies.

Breaking News

Nothing grabs the attention of C-suite executives more effectively than talk of profits, which explains the current buzz around predictive maintenance.

Geeks and gearheads across the landscape of heavy industry have been hearing the siren song of predictive maintenance for decades. The basic idea is simple: with the right blend of math and sensors, machines are fixed before they break, valuable resources are spared, and unplanned downtime is rendered obsolete. But until recently, the processes that would have made predictive maintenance possible either didn't exist or were far too expensive to be considered practical.

Today, the situation looks different. The combination of advanced analytics, low-cost sensors, and the Internet of Things (IoT) promises to elevate maintenance from a cost center to a profit center. True believers like Mark Grabb, the technology leader for analytics at GE Software, see predictive maintenance as a spark with the power to ignite an economic revolution (*http://linkd.in/1LmFzVu*).

From his perspective, broader adoption of predictive maintenance principles will enable companies to provide a far wider range of products and services than ever before. Early adopters are likely to be companies in the energy, transportation, manufacturing, and information technology sectors. As more parts of the economy become dependent on services and benefits flowing through the IoT, the appeal of predictive maintenance will spread rapidly.

Looking at the Numbers

A seminal study[1] by the US Department of Energy's Pacific Northwest National Laboratory claimed that a "functional predictive

---

1 "Operations & Maintenance Best Practices: A Guide to Achieving Operational Efficiency," (*http://1.usa.gov/1DcOa7i*) US Department of Energy Federal Energy Management Program, August 2010.

---

maintenance program" can reduce maintenance cost by 30 percent, reduce downtime by 45 percent, and eliminate breakdowns by as much as 75 percent.

According to the report:

> The advantages of predictive maintenance are many. A well-orchestrated predictive maintenance program will all but eliminate catastrophic equipment failures. We will be able to schedule maintenance activities to minimize or delete overtime cost. We will be able to minimize inventory and order parts, as required, well ahead of time to support the downstream maintenance needs. We can optimize the operation of the equipment, saving energy cost and increasing plant reliability.

If maintenance makes the leap from the garage to the C-suite, it will follow paths that were pioneered years ago by drab back-office functions such as accounting, which evolved into finance and is led by CFOs; and data processing, which evolved into IT and is led by CIOs.

Is this the dawning of the Age of Predictive Maintenance? Mike Hitmar, a global product marketing manager at SAS who specializes in manufacturing, offers a "resounding yes" to that question. "Analytics are cool now, and people are beginning to develop a better understanding of what analytics can do," he says. "Analytics are the flipside of BI (business intelligence). Instead of looking backward at what's already happened, you're looking forward and anticipating what's likely to happen."

The economic potential of predictive maintenance—not wearable technology or connected refrigerators—will drive steady growth of the IoT, Hitmar says. Companies like GE, Cisco, IBM, and Intel are counting on predictive maintenance capabilities enabled by the IoT to create an additional $100 billion in value for the energy and utilities industries by 2020. According to Gartner,[2] the IoT will create nearly $2 trillion in new value across the global economy during the next five years, and much of the value creation will be spurred by predictive maintenance.

---

2 "Forecast: The Internet of Things, Worldwide, 2013," (*http://gtnr.it/1BAx4Rr*), Middleton, Peter, Peter Kjeldsen, and Jim Tully. 2013. *Gartner, Inc.*, November 2013.

Ganesh Bell, chief digital officer and general manager at GE Power & Water, sees three layers of value creation from predictive maintenance strategies, as outlined in Table 8-1.

Table 8-1. Multilayer approach to predictive maintenance

Organizational Layer	Focus	Goal
C-suite	Market performance	Optimize corporate profitability
VPs	Operational optimization	Increase efficiency; lower overall operating costs
Managers	Asset performance	Increase asset reliability and availability; reduce maintenance costs

Describing the first layer, he says:

> For plant managers and maintenance managers, the primary focus will be asset performance. Their goal is zero unplanned downtime for every asset they have. That's the foundation—increasing the reliability and availability of assets while lowering maintenance costs.

Bell adds, "The next layer are the VPs, who are thinking in terms of optimizing the entire plant operation, not just the physical assets, but everything, including the supply chain and human resources."

The third and highest layer is the C-suite, which focuses on optimizing profitability across the enterprise. "In the energy sector, when we talk about a 1 percent fuel savings, it translates into about $65 billion in value for our customers," he says. "From our perspective, we see predictive maintenance having a significant business impact at all three layers."

Each layer has different perspectives and goals. At the bottom layer, it's essential for managers and operators to understand the physics of individual parts and machines. At the next layer, the interplay between resources, machines, processes, and human behavior is critical. At the topmost layer, the focus is on making sure that the efficiencies achieved at the lower layers add up to market advantages and real profits.

Clearly, predictive maintenance is more than a tool or a solution; it's an integrated business strategy, with multiple layers, interconnected processes, and complex relationships among various stakeholders across the enterprise and beyond its traditional boundaries.

Bell says he sees similarities between the evolution of predictive maintenance and the evolution of ERP, CRM, supply chain management, and other systems that have become indispensable staples of the corporate IT portfolio. "We're already seeing CIOs getting involved in this and partnering with the head of assets or the head of operations at their companies to build up the IT infrastructure necessary to support predictive maintenance," he says.

It's important for CIOs to stretch beyond their traditional roles as "digitizers" when they prepare IT for the shift to predictive maintenance, he adds. "Predictive maintenance isn't the same as replacing atoms with electrons or using software to perform business processes. This is something fundamentally different; it's about creating new value and new revenue for the company."

Preventive Versus Predictive

The difference between *preventive maintenance* and *predictive maintenance* is more than merely semantic. Imagine a pyramid with three levels. At the bottom is *reactive maintenance*, where the operative philosophy is "wait until it breaks and then fix it." The next level up is preventive maintenance, in which repairs or alterations are made at scheduled intervals. The goal of preventive maintenance is extending the useful life of machines and their parts.

At the top of our imaginary pyramid is predictive maintenance, which seeks to stave off problems before they occur. In predictive maintenance scenarios, the goal is eliminating unplanned outages or breakdowns entirely. It's not hard to see why utility companies are leaders in predictive maintenance: power outages are expensive to remedy, create a variety of real dangers, and are guaranteed to anger customers. Medical device manufacturers are also at the vanguard of predictive maintenance, for similar reasons.

Based on information from the DOE, Tables 8-2 and 8-3 show key differences between preventive and predictive maintenance.

Table 8-2. Advantages of preventive maintenance and predictive maintenance

Preventive maintenance	Predictive maintenance
Cost-effective in many capital-intensive processes	Increased component operational life/availability
Flexibility allows for the adjustment of maintenance periodicity	Allows for preemptive corrective actions
Increased component life cycle	Decrease in equipment or process downtime
Energy savings	Decrease in costs for parts and labor
Reduced equipment or process failure	Better product quality
Estimated 12% to 18% cost savings over reactive maintenance program	Improved worker and environmental safety
	Improved worker morale
	Energy savings
	Estimated 8% to 12% cost savings over preventive maintenance program

Table 8-3. Disadvantages of preventive maintenance and predictive maintenance

Preventive maintenance	Predictive maintenance
Catastrophic failures still likely to occur	Increased investment in diagnostic equipment
Labor intensive	Increased investment in staff training
Includes performance of unneeded maintenance	Savings potential not readily seen by management
Potential for incidental damage to components in conducting unneeded maintenance	

Follow the Money

Greg Fell is the former CIO of Terex, a heavy equipment manufacturer. Previously, he held technology management roles at Ford Motor Company. Fell believes the practical and economic arguments in favor of predictive maintenance have become too powerful to ignore.

"The best way of thinking about predictive maintenance is by tying it into a revenue stream," he says:

> When your machines are up and running, you're making money. When your machines are down, you're losing money. A typical automobile manufacturer can produce a car every 60 seconds. If retail value of each car is $40,000, your gains or losses add up very quickly.

While preventive maintenance relies on the straightforward concept of "mean time between failure" to create practical maintenance schedules, predictive maintenance is based on a deeper and more fundamental understanding of the physics underlying the operations of machines and their various parts.

"Instead of just looking at the average time between failures, you're looking for subtle clues within the machine itself," Fell says. "You're measuring sound, heat, vibration, tilt, acceleration, compression, humidity, and checking to see if any of those are out of spec." Fell adds:

> The basic idea of predictive maintenance isn't new. What's changed is that it's much less expensive to get data off a machine today than it was in the past. Twenty years ago, an accelerometer cost thousands of dollars. Today, every smartphone has one built into it. The technology required for predictive maintenance has been miniaturized, and the cost has fallen dramatically.

The cost of transmitting data from machines to data repositories has also fallen. In the past, operational data generated by a machine was collected manually by a technician on the shop floor. Today, that data can be sent wirelessly to the Internet via Bluetooth or WiFi.

Not All Work Is Created Equal

Another problem facing traditional preventive maintenance scenarios is the assumption that every machine of a certain type will be operated under similar conditions or within similar parameters. Clifton Triplett is managing partner of SteelePointe Partners, a management consulting firm. He is also a former CIO at Baker Hughes, a $20 billion global oil field services business, and manufacturing process executive at General Motors. A West Point graduate, Triplett knows firsthand that equipment is often operated in situations and circumstances that can be unforeseen by the design engineer or manufacturer.

"It's important to remember that not all work is created equal," Triplett says. "If you run a tool within its designed operating constraints, it will require a certain level of maintenance. But if you run it outside, well under or over normal operating specifications, a different level of service is generally going to be optimal."

For example, a truck designed primarily to deliver mineral ore in Canada will require a different level of service if it's used to haul ore up and down mountains, on flat paved roads, or across dirt roads in a hot, dusty desert. In the oil and gas business, a drill bit primarily used in conventional "straight down" drilling operations will require different reliability parameters and service requirements when compared to a bit being utilized in more challenging unconventional horizontal drilling. Reliability is in part defined by design, but reusable equipment is highly dependent upon the maintenance services performed on it.

"In the military, we would run tools and equipment in as many different scenarios as possible to understand how they would perform and react to the different environments," Triplett says:

> We would test equipment at various altitudes, temperatures, and levels of humidity. We would test equipment to see whether freshwater or saltwater would affect its performance. You name it, we tried it and we assessed how we should adapt our maintenance schedule to adapt to the conditions we place our equipment.

Companies that emulate the military's attention to maintenance issues can charge a premium for their services. For example, as drilling conditions become more extreme, the value of reliability grows. If you're an independent oil driller and you have a great predictive maintenance program in place (assuming it's proven by reliability metrics and performance), it is possible to demand higher service charges or take on more challenging opportunities. Nonproductive time (NPT) is the "evil all drilling companies seek to eliminate," Triplett says. Service or operating failures are the No. 1 contributor to NPT, and trust in the maintenance program of service companies builds confidence in the minds of the customers when awarding work.

"Oilfield operators are also more likely to let you use existing equipment longer if they trust your maintenance program, since they will worry less about it breaking down," Triplett says. "If you have a poor maintenance strategy or record, they're more likely to demand that you use new equipment every time you start drilling. Being forced to always use new tooling can be incredibly expensive, and most likely noncompetitive."

Smart operators understand that predictive maintenance translates into pricing power and now, with more complex drilling techniques, a large market share opportunity. Halliburton, for example, has developed a reputation for being able to perform reliably in high temperature environments longer than its competitors. That reputation creates pricing power and generates higher profits.

Building a Foundation

Daniel Koffler is chief technology officer at Rio Tinto Alcan (RTA), the global leader in the aluminum business and one of five product groups operated by Rio Tinto Group, a multinational metals and mining company. RTA annually produces 31.4 million tons of bauxite, 7 million tons of alumina (aluminum oxide), and 2.2 million tons of primary aluminum. Koffler is responsible for making sure that RTA's machinery keeps running.

"There's inherent downtime in any sort of run-to-fail scenario. And you're forced into keeping extra assets on hand to pick up the slack when your primary assets fail," Koffler says. "Either way, you're losing production capacity during the repair time, and you're spending money on extra assets that are sitting idle."

Although a scheduled maintenance model allows you to avoid unplanned downtime, there's also a good chance you'll end up repairing equipment or replacing parts unnecessarily. "With a predictive maintenance model, we can keep assets running longer *and* we avoid unscheduled downtime," Koffler says.

According to Koffler, reliable data and a solid computational model are foundational to predictive maintenance. Additionally, the corporate culture must adjust to a process that doesn't always yield perfect results.

"At the management level, people need to accept that a data model doesn't start at 100 percent maturity. It's a process that takes time. You're not going to start at the peak," Koffler says. "That means you have to accept additional risk. There may be unexpected failures. They are part of the process."

Koffler stresses that predictive maintenance isn't a magical formula; it's an iterative, scientific process that builds slowly to maturity:

> You need collaboration between subject matter experts such as mechanics and data scientists. The mechanic understands how the machinery works, and the data scientist knows how to build a data model. The mechanic's knowledge should be codified into the data model. The mechanic and the data scientist need to communicate over a period of time to refine the model. There's no way to do this without cross-functional collaboration.

Like any process based on statistical analysis, predictive maintenance is inherently imprecise. The risk posed by predictive strategies must be "negotiated" and understood by the stakeholders involved, he says:

> You may want to negotiate an ultra-conservative approach where you're changing a part earlier, but you're still maximizing value by pushing the part closer to its predicted failure. Then it would be a discussion about risk, not about analytics. Those kinds of discussions—about cost, productivity, and risk—happen every day in business. It's the nature of real life.

Koffler isn't convinced that predictive analytics will become a mainstream consumer product in the near future. "You'd have to do the cost-benefit analysis. Placing sensors, collecting data, analyzing data —it all costs money," he says. "Just because you can do something doesn't mean you have to do it. Take the belts in the engine of your car, for instance. You could put sensors on the belts, but it makes more sense economically to run them until they break, and then replace them."

It's Not All About Heavy Machinery

Not every aspect of predictive maintenance revolves around heavy machinery and industrial processes. Doug Sauder leads the research and development team at Precision Planting, a company that makes technologies that help farmers improve seed spacing, depth, and root systems in their fields.

"The agricultural challenges of the future are all about doing more with less in a sustainable way," Sauder says. "It's about meeting the demands of a growing population and being environmentally responsible." From his perspective, predictive analytics play an absolutely critical role in any reasonable solution.

"We can be smarter about maximizing every square inch of ground, everything from what kinds of seeds to plant, how many seeds, planting the seeds properly, watering the seeds, and applying just the right amount of fertilizer," Sauder says:

> For example, it's important to model the nitrogen in a field. You need to model the rainfall and understand how it disperses into the ground. You need the ability to predict where the nitrogen is moving so you can tell when it's time to apply more nitrogen to the field.

Sauder and his team not only help farmers understand more about their fields, but also "train" farm equipment to perform better. "We call it 'smart iron,' and it's essentially technology that allows the farmer's equipment to think for itself as it's going through a field," he says.

From the air, all corn fields look fairly similar. But at the ground level, every field is unique. When a corn planter travels through a field, it continually encounters a range of soil conditions. Some soil is hard; some soil is soft. If the planting pressure on the equipment is static, some seeds will be deposited deeper than others, resulting in uneven growth. But the farmer won't discover the problem until months later, and by then it will be too late to fix.

Sauder says:

> We put sensors on the planters that take hundreds of measurements per second. We can vary the pressure in real time as the planter goes through the field to make sure that every seed goes into the sweet spot. With "smart iron," we can literally micromanage every bit of the field and make certain that every seed is dropped into the right environment.

The ability to "micromanage" a cornfield requires the same blend of predictive capabilities needed to manage the performance of gas turbines, jet engines, nuclear generators, diesel locomotives, ore haulers, and magnetic resonance imaging devices. As Koffler suggests earlier in this report, predictive maintenance is a multidisciplinary science, with roots and branches extending far beyond heavy industry.

The Future of Maintenance

The next steps in the evolution of predictive maintenance are likely to involve heavier doses of machine learning and closed-loop automation technologies. For the moment, predictive maintenance systems are limited to sending up red flags and issuing alerts of impeding failure. Future versions will undoubtedly include high-level decisioning tools and recommendation engines.

Prakash Seshadri, product development head at Mu Sigma, sees predictive maintenance evolving inevitably into prescriptive maintenance. In a prescriptive maintenance scenario, the system won't just tell you that something bad is about to happen; it will offer helpful recommendations.

"It will go beyond saying, 'There's a likelihood this will break,'" Seshadri says:

> A predictive maintenance system will say, "Based on current and expected conditions, here's what you should do" and offer a range of choices, thereby guiding the human to make better decisions. But at the same time, if the human decides to override the recommendations, the system will capture that behavior and evolve through learning.

Today, predictive maintenance is practiced largely within the IT, manufacturing, healthcare, and energy sectors. In the near future, predictive maintenance will become more widely adopted in the retail, telecom, media, and finance industries. The potential for cross-pollination seems unlimited.

CHAPTER 9

Can Data Security and Rapid Business Innovation Coexist?

Topline Summary

It's difficult to be creative when someone's looking over your shoulder. Is it really possible to strike a balance between innovation, security, governance, and compliance? Interviews with experts from a variety of industries suggest that achieving a balance is possible, but difficult. Some observers believe that balance is the wrong word, since it implies a state in which all parties are equally satisfied. The proper goal, they say, is harmony.

In many ways, the quest for balance or harmony reflects the immaturity of big data culture. To paraphrase one source in this report, nobody expected big data to catch on as quickly as it did, and as a result, few organizations took the time to think through the consequences of shifting from older to newer styles of data management. For better or worse, the transition has proved revolutionary.

This report was written in the autumn of 2014 and released at the O'Reilly Strata + Hadoop World conference at the Javits Center in New York City.

Finding a Balance

During the final decade of the 20th century and the first decade of the 21st century, many companies learned the hard way that launching an ERP system was more than a matter of acquiring new technology. Successful ERP deployments, it turned out, also required hiring new people and developing new processes.

After a series of multimillion-dollar misadventures at major corporations, it became apparent that ERP was not something you simply bought, took home, and plugged in. "People, process, and technology" became the official mantra of ERP implementations. CIOs became "change management leaders" and stepped gingerly into the unfamiliar zone of business process transformation. They also began hiring people with business backgrounds to serve alongside the hardcore techies in their IT organizations.

As quickly as the lessons of ERP were learned, they were forgotten. In an eerie rewinding of history, companies are now learning painfully similar lessons about big data. The peculiar feeling of déjà vu is especially palpable at the junction where big data meets data security.

There is a significant difference, however, between what happened in the past and what's happening now. When a company's ERP transformation went south, the CIO was fired and another CIO was hired to finish the job. When the contents of a data warehouse are compromised, the impact is considerably more widespread, and the potential for something genuinely nasty occurring is much higher. If ERP was like dynamite, big data is like plutonium.

"Security is tricky. Any small weakness can become a major problem once the hackers find a way to leverage it," says Edouard Servan-Schreiber, director for solution architecture at MongoDB, a popular NoSQL database management system. "You can come up with a mathematically elegant security infrastructure, but the main challenge is adherence to a very strict security process. That's the issue. More and more, a single mistake is a fatal mistake."

The velocity of change is part of the problem. It's fair to say that relatively few people anticipated the short amount of time it would take for big data to go mainstream. As a result, the technology part of big data is far ahead of the people and process parts.

"We've all seen hype roll through our industry," says Jon M. Deutsch, president of The Data Warehouse Institute (TDWI) for New York, Connecticut, and New Jersey. "Usually it takes years for the hype to become reality. Big data is an exception to that rule."

Many TDWI members "have the technology ingredients of big data in place," says Deutsch, despite the lack of standard methods and protocols for implementing big data projects.

In tightly regulated industries such as financial services and pharmaceuticals, the lack of clear standards has slowed the adoption of big data systems. Concerns about security and privacy, says Deutsch, "limit the scope of big data projects, inject uncertainty, and restrict deployment."

A general perception that big data frameworks such as Hadoop are less secure than "old-fashioned" relational database technology also contributes to the sense of hesitancy. Hadoop and NoSQL are playing catch-up with traditional SQL database products.

"We're bringing the security of the Apache Hadoop stack up to the levels of the traditional database," says Charles Zedlewski, vice president of products at Cloudera, a pioneer in Hadoop data management systems. "We're adding key enterprise security elements such as RBAC and encryption in a consistent way across the platform." For example, the Cloudera Enterprise Data Hub "includes Apache Sentry, an open source project we cofounded, to provide unified role-based authorization for the platform. We've also developed Cloudera Navigator to provide audit and lineage capabilities."

Unscrambling the Eggs

Clearly, many businesses see a competitive advantage in ramping up their big data capabilities. At the same time, they are hesitant about diving into the deep end of the big data pool without assurances they won't see their names in headlines about breached security. It's no secret that when Hadoop and other nontraditional data management frameworks were invented, data security was not high on the list of operational priorities. Perhaps, as Jon Deutsch suggested earlier, no one seriously expected big data to become such a big deal in such a short span of time.

Suddenly, we're in the same predicament as Aladdin. The genie is out of the bottle. He's powerful and dangerous. We want our three wishes, but we have to wish carefully or something bad could happen…

"Big data analytics software is about crunching data and returning the answers to queries very quickly," says Terence Craig, founder and CTO of PatternBuilders, a streaming analytics vendor. He is also coauthor of *Privacy and Big Data* (O'Reilly). "As long as we want those primary capabilities, it will be difficult to put restrictions on the technology."

Is it possible to achieve a fair balance between the need for data security and the need for rapid business innovation? Can the desire for privacy coexist with the desire for an ever-widening array of choices for consumers? Is there a way to protect information while distributing insights gleaned from that information?

"Data security and innovation are not at loggerheads," says Tony Baer, principal analyst at Ovum, a global technology research and advisory firm. "In fact, I would suggest they are in alignment." Baer, a veteran observer of the tech industry, says the real challenges are knowing where the data came from and keeping track of who's using it.

"Previously, you were dealing with data that was from your internal systems. You probably knew the lineage of that data—who collected it, how it was collected, under what conditions, with what restrictions, and what you can do with it," he says. "The difference with big data is that in many cases you're harvesting data from external sources over which you have no control. Your awareness of the provenance of that data is going to be highly variable and limited."

Some of the big data you vacuum up might have been "collected under conditions that do not necessarily reflect your own internal policies," says Baer. Then you will be faced with a difficult choice, something akin to the prisoner's dilemma: using the data might violate your company's governance policies or break the rules of a regulatory body that oversees your industry. On the other hand, not using the data might create a business advantage for your competitors. It's a slippery slope, replete with ambiguity and uncertainty.

At minimum, you need processes for protecting the data and ensuring its integrity. Even the simplest database can be protected with a three-step process of authentication, authorization, and access control:[1]

---

[1] "Oracle Fusion Middleware Administrator's Guide for Oracle HTTP Server" (*http://bit.ly/1Bvf6PS*)

- Authentication verifies that a user is who they say they are.

- Authorization determines if a user is permitted to use a particular kind of data resource.

- Access control determines when, where, and how users can access the data resource.

Ensuring the integrity of your data requires keeping track of who's using it, where it's being used, and what it's being used for. Software for automating the various steps of data security is readily available. The key to maintaining data security, however, isn't software—it's a relentless focus on discipline and accountability.

"It boils down to having the right policies and processes in place to manage and control access to the data. For instance, organizations need to understand exactly what big data is contained within the enterprise and where, and assess any legal or regulatory need to safeguard the data. This could range from interactions with customers over social networks, to transaction data from online purchases," says Joanna Belbey, a compliance expert at Actiance, a firm that helps companies use various communications channels (for example, email, unified communications, instant messages, collaboration tools, social media) while meeting regulatory, legal, and corporate compliance requirements.

Depending on the situation, approaches to data security can vary. "The trade-offs you make when you're going after a market or you're doing something new might be different from the trade-offs you make for security when you're a major bank, for example. You have to negotiate those trade-offs through an exercise in good, solid risk management," says Gary McGraw, CTO at software security firm Cigital and author of *Software Security* (*http://amzn.to/1it7PM2*) (Addison-Wesley).

"I don't think that a startup has to follow the same risk-management regimen as a bank. A startup can approach the problem of security as a risk-management exercise, and most startups that I advise do exactly that," says McGraw. "They make trade-offs between speed, agility, and engineering, which is OK because they are startups."

Avoiding the "NoSQL, No Security" Cop-Out

The knock against nontraditional data management technologies such as Hadoop and NoSQL is their relative lack of built-in data security features. As a result, companies that opt for newer database technologies are forced to deal with data security at the application level, which places an unreasonable burden on the shoulders of developers who are paid to deliver innovation, not security. Traditional database vendors have used the immaturity of nontraditional data management frameworks and systems to spread FUD—fear, uncertainty, and doubt—about products based on Hadoop and NoSQL.

Not surprisingly, vendors of products and services based on the newer database technologies disagree strenuously with arguments that Hadoop and NoSQL pose unmanageable security risks for competitive business organizations.

"Business is going to change, and the regulations on business are going to change. NoSQL databases have gained traction because they offer flexibility and fast development of applications without sacrificing reliability and security," says Alicia C. Saia, director, solutions marketing at MarkLogic, an enterprise-level NoSQL database based on proprietary code.

Saia flat-out rejected the notion that security and rapid innovation are mutually exclusive conditions in a modern data management environment. "When you're running a business, you want to innovate as quickly as possible. It can take 18 months to model a relational database, which is an unacceptably long time frame in today's fast-paced economy," she says.

Providers of traditional database technology "want to frame this as a binary choice between innovation and security," says Saia. "One of the great advantages of an enterprise NoSQL database is that it's flexible, which means you can respond to the inevitable external shocks without spending millions of dollars breaking apart and reassembling a traditional database to accommodate new kinds of data."

MarkLogic leverages the combination of security and innovation as an element of its marketing strategy, noting that it offers "higher security certifications than any NoSQL database—providing certified, fine-grained, government-grade security at the database level."

"You don't want to be forced to choose between security and innovation," says Saia. "You want a foundational database that has a layer of stringent security built into it so you're not in situations where every new application needs its own security. Ideally, you should be able to develop as many applications as you need without stressing over data security."

Saia and her team came up with a seven-point "checklist" of reasonable expectations for database security in modern data management environments:

1. You should not have to choose between data security and innovation.

2. Your database should never be a weak point for data security, data integrity, or data governance.

3. Your database should support your application security needs, not the other way around.

4. A flexible, schema-agnostic database will make it faster and cheaper to respond to regulatory changes and inquiries.

5. Your enterprise data will expand and change over time, so pick a database that makes integration easier—and that lets you scale up and down as needed.

6. Your database should manage data seamlessly across storage tiers, in real time.

7. NoSQL does not have to mean No ACID,[2] No Security, No HA/DR,[3] or No Auditing.

Anonymize This!

For some companies, security depends on anonymity—the companies aren't anonymous, but they make sure the data they use has been scrubbed of personally identifiable information (PII).

"How do we bake security into our approach? Our fundamental conception is that it's not about the data, it's about the signals," says Laks Srinivasan, co-COO at Opera Solutions, an analytics-as-a-

---

2 ACID is an acronym for Atomicity, Consistency, Isolation, and Durability.

3 HA/DR stands for High Availability/Disaster Recovery.

service provider that works with major financial institutions, air-lines, and communications companies. "We look for patterns in the data. We extract those patterns, which we call signals, and use them to drive the data science and BI. That mitigates the risk in a big way because people aren't carrying raw customer data around in their laptops."

Most users don't need or even want to deal with raw data, he says. "We extract the juice from terabytes of data. We detach the PII from the behavior patterns, and we make the signals available to data scientists. That's what they're really interested in."

Focusing on signals instead of data "doesn't solve all the issues, but it reduces the proliferation of data and lowers the likelihood of incidents in which personal data is accidentally released," he says.

Decoupling data from PII provides a measure of safety for all parties involved: consumers who generate data, companies that collect data, and firms that analyze data to harvest usable insights. DataSong, for example, is a San Francisco-based startup that onboards data from its customers (multi- and omni-channel retailers) and measures the incremental effectiveness of their marketing activities. "Our customers give us mountains of data, such as ad impressions, click streams, emails, e-commerce transactions, and in-store orders. It's a lot of data, and keeping it secure is very important," says John Wallace, the company's founder and CEO.

DataSong deals with the security issue by analyzing only data that has been stripped of PII. "We bake data security into the engagement rather than into the technology," says Wallace.

Data science providers like Opera Solutions and DataSong operate on the principle that anonymized data can be more valuable than personally identifiable data. If that's true, then why all the fuss over data security? Part of the discomfort arises from the "creepiness factor" we experience when a marketer crosses the invisible line between knowing enough and knowing too much about our interests.

Here's a typical example: you search for a topic such as "back pain," and the next time you launch your web browser, whatever page you open is strewn with ads for painkillers. Here's another scenario: you're looking for a present, let's say jewelry, for a special someone. You walk away from your computer and that special someone sits down to check her email—and she sees page after page of ads for jewelry. The possibilities for embarrassment are virtually unlimited.

Both of those examples are fairly benign. In *Who Owns the Future* (*http://amzn.to/1iIS4kP*) (Simon & Schuster), computer scientist and composer Jaron Lanier wrote that "a surveillance economy is neither sustainable nor democratic," and that we gradually become less free as we "share" our personal information with a virtual cartel of "private spying" services that feeds on the data we generate every time we log on to a computer or use a mobile device. "This triumph of consumer passivity over empowerment is heartbreaking," he wrote.

"We as individuals who want to live in a fully digital world need to come to grips with the fact that we are no longer going to be able to have privacy in any sense of the way we had it before," says Terence Craig. "Even if the corporations behave, even if all the government actors behave, there will still be external actors or extra-legal actors who will penetrate systems and use information to generate revenue or power in some way. That's the nature of the beast."

"We're creating a society that requires everyone to have a digital persona," says Craig. "In the Internet age, privacy has been thrown away for efficiency—and not even deliberately, in most cases. The accelerating adoption of the Internet of Things and streaming analytics solutions like PatternBuilders (*http://bit.ly/1uxOyKI*) will make it possible to breach privacy in unexpected and unintentional ways. But both IOT and streaming analytics are so relatively new that it is hard to predict either the costs or the benefits of having real-time access to IOT devices beyond your cell phone: glucose monitors, brain wave monitors, etc. This is where things will get really interesting."

As a society, Craig says, we should begin looking seriously at regulations that would limit or curtail data retention. "Almost all of the worst-case scenarios involve data retention," he says. "If you need real-time data to catch a terrorist, then great, go ahead and save the data you need to do that."

If you're not actively involved in rooting out terrorists or averting threats to public safety, however, you should be required at regular intervals to expunge any data you collect. "I could care less if Google knows that I like Crest toothpaste and my wife likes Tom's of Maine natural toothpaste. The big issue is the collation of data, keeping it for an extended period of time, and building up individual profiles of a large percentage of the population," says Craig.

Specifically, Craig is concerned about the capability of governments to collect and analyze data. When governments fall, either through democratic or nondemocratic processes, their records become the property of new governments. "Hopefully, the people who get the records will be responsible people," he says. "But history has shown that good leadership doesn't last forever. Sooner or later, a bad leader turns up. Do we really want to hand over an NSA-level data infrastructure to the next Pol Pot?"

Replacing Guidance with Rules

Comprehensive regulations around data management would help, according to Dale Meyerrose, a retired US Air Force major general and former CIO for the US Intelligence Community. "If the government can create comprehensive rules and standards for work safety such as OSHA (Occupational Safety and Health Act), it can certainly create rules and standards for data security," says Meyerrose.

Too many of the guidelines around data security are just that: guidelines, not laws or regulations. "How seriously will anyone take a voluntary set of standards? The role of government is creating policies and laws. If you give companies a choice, they're not going to choose spending more money than their competitors on something they aren't legally required to do," he says.

Like most of the sources interviewed for this paper, Meyerrose sees no inherent conflict between security and innovation. "In the past, you put your ideas on a piece of paper and locked it in a safe behind your desk. Today, it's in a database. The only thing that's changed is the medium," he says. "So it's not really a matter of cybersecurity or network security or computer security. It's just security, and security is something you can control."

From Meyerrose's perspective, cybersecurity is "an ecosystem of multiple supply chains—a human resources supply chain, an operational processes supply chain, and a technology supply chain." Each of those supply chains must be carefully scrutinized and vetted for trust.

"I find it amazing that we can get the technical part right and get the human part wrong. In the case of Edward Snowden, there was no technical malfunction. But the process wasn't designed to handle a complicit insider," says Meyerrose.

Jeffrey Carr is the author of *Inside Cyber Warfare: Mapping the Cyber Underworld* (O'Reilly) and is an adjunct professor at George Washington University. He is the founder of the cybersecurity consultancy Taia Global, as well as the Suits and Spooks security conference.

In a 2014 paper, "The Classification of Valuable Data in an Assumption of Breach Paradigm," (*http://bit.ly/ZigmIb*) Carr wrote that since adversaries eventually figure out ways of breaching even the best security systems, responsible organizations "must identify which data is worth protecting and which is not."

Rather than fretting over the possibility of something bad happening, organizations should prepare for the worst. "Executives need to realize that if they're in an industry that involves high tech, finance, energy, or anything related to weapons or the military, they're in a state of perpetual breach," says Carr. "That's the first thing you need to come to grips with. You will never be secure. Once you've reached that realization, you should identify your most valuable digital assets—your 'crown jewels'—and do your best to protect them."

Carr recommends that companies take stock of their digital assets and objectively rank their value to hackers. "Remember, it doesn't matter what *you* think is valuable. What matters is what a potential adversary thinks is valuable," says Carr. For example, if your company is developing cutting-edge software for a new kind of industrial robot, it would be reasonable to expect attacks from organizations—and even countries—that are working on similar software.

"Lots of executives are still looking for a silver bullet that will protect their networks, but that's not realistic," says Carr, who predicted that more companies would begin taking security challenges seriously "when the SEC (Security Exchange Commission) makes it a rule instead of a guidance."

Like Meyerrose, he says that process is a critical part of the solution. "You can make it harder for an adversary to gain access to your crown jewels. Part of making it harder is training your employees to spot spear phishing attacks, meaning train them to look at their email and say, 'There's something about this email that doesn't look right; I'm not going to click on the link, open the attachment. I'll pick up the phone and call the person that sent it to me to confirm that it's legitimate.' Training is a positive thing that makes it harder for potential bad guys to harm you. It won't keep a dedicated adversary off your network. They'll just find a way in eventually, if they have enough time and money to do that."

Training is a key piece of "cyber hygiene," Carr says. "It's like putting chlorine in a swimming pool. It will keep you from catching some low-grade infection, but it won't protect you from sharks."

Not to Pass the Buck, but...

Although it won't eradicate the problem, clarifying the regulations around data security would definitely help. "There is no one central set of regulations covering data security and privacy within the US. It's pretty much a patchwork quilt at this point," Joanna Belbey wrote in an email. "And while privacy concerns are being addressed through regulation in some sectors—for example, the Federal Communications Commission (FCC) works with telecommunications companies, the Health Insurance Portability and Accountability Act (HIPAA) addresses healthcare data, Public Utility Commissions (PUC) in several states restrict the use of smart grid data, and the Federal Trade Commission (FTC) is developing guidelines for web activity—all this activity has been broad in system coverage and open to interpretation in most cases."

That sounds like a call for legislative action at the national level. A unified national data security policy would undoubtedly remove some of the uncertainty and create a set of common standards.

At the same time, it seems likely that many of the security issues associated with Hadoop and NoSQL will be resolved within a reasonably short period of time by good old-fashioned market forces. Heartbleed, the OpenSSL bug, cast a spotlight on the kind of problems that can arise when the software industry relies on the volunteer open source community to perform major miracles on miniscule or nonexistent budgets. Vendors that want to compete in the big data space will figure out how to bring their products up to snuff, and they'll pass the development costs along to their customers. Eventually, consumers will foot the bill, but the costs will be spread so thinly that few of us will notice.

"The answer is that you've got to pay for security," says Gary McGraw, adding that it is unfair and unrealistic to expect the open source community to do the job for free. "The demand for talent is too high and everybody with experience in this field is already incredibly busy."

CHAPTER 10

The Last Mile of Analytics: Making the Leap from Platforms to Tools

Topline Summary

Technology innovation tends to proceed from the inside out. The early stages of invention usually focus on getting the most basic aspects of the new technology to work without falling apart. Then the innovation tends to move outward. The basic technology is buried under or hidden behind a user interface.

The development of advanced analytics is following a similar path. Processes and techniques that initially required highly specialized knowledge and training are gradually being replaced by tools that are considerably less powerful, but much more usable. Some are calling this stage "the last mile of analytics," while others refer to it as the "verticalization of analytics." No matter what you call it, the trend seems fairly clear: analytics have entered a more mature phase. More companies are building analytics with an end user in mind, and hoping to profit from the growing belief that analytics are critical to business growth in modern markets.

This report, written in the summer of 2014, looks at advanced analytics and machine learning from the perspective of entrepreneurs and investors who are eager to monetize data science and expand into new markets.

Inching Closer to the Front Lines

Models are fine if you're a data scientist, but when you're looking for insights that translate into meaningful actions and real business results, what you really need are better tools. The first generation of big data analytics vendors focused on creating platforms for modelers and developers. Now a new generation of vendors is focusing on delivering advanced analytics directly to business users.

This new generation of vendors is following the broader business market, which is more interested in deployment and less interested in development. Now that analytics are considered more normal than novel, success is measured in terms of usability and rates of adoption. Interestingly, the user base isn't entirely human: the newest generation of analytics must also work and play well with closed-loop decisioning systems, which are largely automated.

This is a fascinating tale in which the original scientists and innovators of the analytics movement might find themselves elbowed aside by a user community that includes both humans and robots. In some cases, "older" analytics companies are finding themselves losing ground to "younger" analytics companies that understand what users apparently want: tools with advanced analytic capabilities that can be used in real-world business scenarios like fraud detection, credit scoring, customer life cycle analysis, marketing optimization, IT operations, customer support, and more. Since every new software trend needs a label, this one has been dubbed "the last mile of analytics."

The Future Is So Yesterday

In the early days of the automobile, most of the innovation revolved around the power plant as shown in Figure 10-1. After the engine was deemed reliable, the circle of innovation expanded, and features such as brakes, steering wheels, windshield wipers, leather upholstery, and automatic transmissions emerged.

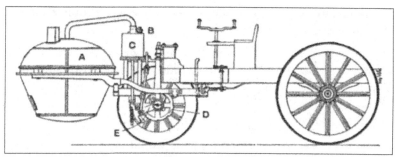

*Figure 10-1. Drawing of the Cugnot Steam Trolly, designed in 1769.[1]
As the design shows, early innovation efforts focused on getting the
basics right. Later cars incorporated features such as steering wheels,
windshields, and brakes.*

The evolution of advanced analytics is following a similar path as
the focus of innovation shifts from infrastructure to applications.
What began as a series of tightly focused experiments around a narrow set of core capabilities has grown into an industry with a global
audience.

"This is a pattern that occurs with practically every new and disruptive technology," says Jeff Erhardt, the CEO of Wise.io, a company
that provides machine learning applications used by businesses for
customer experience management, including proactive support,
minimizing churn, predicting customer satisfaction, and identifying
high-value users.

"Think back to the early days of the Internet. Most of the innovation
was focused on infrastructure. There were small groups of sophisticated people doing very cool things, but most people couldn't really
take advantage of the technology," says Erhardt. "Fast-forward in
time, and the technology has matured to the point where any company can use it as a business tool. The Internet began as a science
project, and now we have Facebook and OpenTable."

From Erhardt's perspective, advanced analytics are moving in the
same direction. "They have the potential to become pervasive, but
they need to become accessible to a broader group of users," he says.
"What's happening now is that advanced analytics are moving out

---

1 "Cugnot Steam Trolly" by Paul Nooncree Hasluck. Licensed under public domain via
   Wikimedia Commons.

of the lab and moving into the real world, where people are using them to make better decisions."

Within the analytics community, there is a growing sense that big changes are looming. "We're at an inflection point, brought about largely by the evolution of unsupervised machine learning," says Mark Jaffe, the CEO of Prelert, a firm that provides anomaly-detection analytics for customers with massive data sets.

"Previously, we assumed that humans would define key aspects of the analysis process. But today's problems are vastly different in terms of scale of data and complexity of systems. We can't assume that users have the skills necessary to define how the data should be analyzed."

Advanced analytics incorporate machine learning algorithms, which can run without human supervision and get better over time. Machine learning "opens the analytics world to a virtual explosion of new applications and users," says Jaffe. "We fundamentally believe that advanced analytics have the power to transform our world on a scale that rivals the Internet and smartphones."

Above and Beyond BI

Advanced analytics is not merely business intelligence (BI) on steroids. "BI typically relies on human judgments. It almost always looks backward. Decisions based on BI analysis are made by humans or by systems following rigid business rules," says Erhardt. "Advanced analytics introduces mathematical modeling into the process of identifying patterns and making decisions. It is forward-looking and predictive of the future."

Like BI, advanced analytics can be used for both exploratory data analysis and decision making. But in the case of advanced analytics, an algorithm or a model—not a human—is making the decision.

"It's important to distinguish between classical statistics and machine learning," says Erhardt. "At the highest level, classical statistics relies on a trained expert to formulate and test an ex-ante hypothesis about the relationship between data and outcomes. Machine learning, on the other hand, derives those signals from the data itself."

Since machine learning techniques can be highly dimensional, non-linear, and self-improving over time, they tend to generate results that are qualitatively superior to classical statistics. Until fairly recently, however, the costs of developing and implementing machine learning systems were too high for most business organizations. The current generation of advanced analytics tools gets around that obstacle by focusing carefully on highly specific use cases within tightly defined markets.

"Industry-specific analytics packages can have workflows or templates built into them for designated scenarios, and can also feature industry-specific terminologies," says Andrew Shikiar, vice president of marketing and business development at BigML, which provides a cloud-based machine learning platform enabling "users of all skillsets to quickly create and leverage powerful predictive models."

Drake Pruitt, former CEO at LIONsolver, a platform of self-tuning software geared for the healthcare industry, says specialization can be a competitive advantage. "You understand your customers' workflows and the regulations that are impacting their world," he says. "When you understand the customer's problems on a more intimate level, you can build a better solution."

Companies that provide specialized software for particular industries become part of the social and economic fabric of those industries. As "insiders," they would enjoy competitive advantages over companies that are perceived as "outsiders." Specialization also makes it easier for software companies to market their products and services within specific verticals. A prospective customer is generally more trusting when a supplier has already demonstrated success within the customer's vertical. Although it's not uncommon for suppliers to claim that their products will "work in any environment," most customers are rightfully wary of such claims.

From the supplier's perspective, a potential downside of vertical specialization is "tying your fortunes to the realities of a specific market or industry," says Pruitt. "In the healthcare industry, for example, we're still in the early stages of applying advanced analytics."

That said, investors are gravitating toward enterprise software start-ups that cater to industry verticals. "As we look to the future, it's the verticalized analytics applications which directly touch a user need or pain that get us most excited," says Jake Flomenberg of Accel

Partners, a venture and growth equity firm that was an early investor in companies such as Facebook, Dropbox, Cloudera, Spotify, Etsy, and Kayak.

The big data market, says Flomenberg, is divided into "above-the-line" technologies and "below-the-line" technologies. "We're in the early innings for the above-the-line zone and expect to see increasingly rapid growth there," he says.

As Figure 10-2 shows, the big data stack has split into two main components. Data-as-a-product, data tooling, and data-driven software are considered "above-the-line" technologies, while data platforms, data infrastructure, and management/security are considered "below-the-line" technologies.

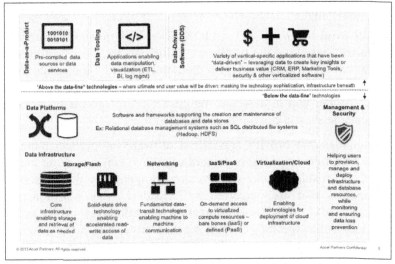

Figure 10-2. As the big data ecosystem expands, "above-the-line" and "below-the-line" technologies are emerging. The fastest growth is expected in the "above-the-line" segment of the market.

"There's room for a couple of winners in data tooling and a couple of winners in data management, but the data-driven software market is up for grabs," he says. "We're talking about hundreds of billions of dollars at stake."

Flomenberg, Ping Li, and Vas Natarajan are coauthors of "The Last Mile in Big Data: How Data Driven Software (DDS) Will Empower the Intelligent Enterprise," a 2013 white paper that examined the likely future of predictive analytics. In the paper, the authors wrote that despite the availability of big data platforms and infrastructure, "few companies have the internal resources required to build…last-mile applications in house. There are not nearly enough analysts and data scientists to meet this demand, and only so many can be trained each year."

Concluding that "software is a far more scalable solution," the authors made the case for data-driven software products and services that "directly serve business users" whose primary goal is deriving value from big data.

"The last mile of analytics, generally speaking, is software that lets you make use of the scalable data management platforms that are becoming more and more democratized," says Flomenberg. That software, he says, "comes in two flavors. The first flavor is data tools for technically savvy users who know the questions they want to ask. The second flavor is for people who don't necessarily know the questions they want to ask, but who just want to do their jobs or complete a task more efficiently."

The "first flavor" includes software for ETL, machine learning, data visualization, and other processes requiring trained data analysts. The "second flavor" includes software that is more user-friendly and business-oriented—what some people are now calling "the last mile of analytics."

"There's an opportunity now to do something with analytics that's similar to what Facebook did with social networking," says Flomenberg. "When people come to work and pop open an app, they expect it to work like Facebook or Google and efficiently surface the data or insight that they need to get their job done."

Moving into the Mainstream

Slowly but surely, data science and advanced analytics are becoming mainstream phenomena. Just ask any runner with a smartphone to name his or her favorite fitness app—you'll get a lengthy and detailed critique of the latest in wearable sensors and mobile analytics.

"Ten years ago, data science was sitting in the math department; it was part of academia," says T.M. Ravi, cofounder of The Hive, a venture capital and private equity firm that backs big data startups. "Today, you see data science applications emerging across functional areas of the business and multiple industry verticals. In the next five to 10 years, data science will disrupt every industry, resulting in better efficiency, huge new revenue streams, new products and services, and new business models. We're seeing a very rapid evolution."

Table 10-1 shows some of the markets in which use of data science techniques and advanced analytics are expanding or expected to grow significantly.

Table 10-1. Existing or emerging markets for data science and advanced analytics[a]

Business functions	Industry segments
Security	Retail and ecommerce
Data center management	Financial services
Marketing	Advertising, media, and entertainment
Customer service	Manufacturing
Finance and accounting	Healthcare
Social media	Transportation

[a] Source: T.M. Ravi

A major driver of that rapid evolution is the availability of low-cost, large-scale data processing infrastructure, such as Hadoop, MongoDB, Pig, Mahout, and others. "You don't have to be Google or Yahoo! to use big data," says Ravi. "Big data infrastructure has really matured over the past seven or eight years, which means you don't have to be a big player to get in the game. We believe the cost of big data infrastructure is trending toward zero."

Another driver is the spread of expertise. A shared body of knowledge has emerged, and some people who began their careers as academics or hardcore data scientists have become entrepreneurs. Jeremy Achin is a good example of that trend. He spent eight years working for Travelers Insurance, where he was director of research and modeling. "I built everything from pricing models to retention models to marketing models," Achin says. "Pretty much anything you could think of within the insurance industry, I've built a model for it."

At one point, he began wondering if his knowledge could be applied in other industries. In 2012, he and a colleague, Tom DeGodoy, launched DataRobot, a sophisticated platform for helping people build and deploy better and more accurate predictive models. One of the firm's backers wrote that DeGodoy and Achin "could be the Lennon and McCartney of data science."[2]

Achin says the firm's mission is "not to focus on any one type of individual, but to take anyone, at any level of experience, and help them become better at building models. That's the grand goal."

He disagreed with predictions that advanced analytics would eventually become so automated that human input would be unnecessary. "It's a little crazy to think you can take data scientists out of the equation completely. We're not trying to replace data scientists; we're just trying to make their jobs a lot easier and give them more powerful tools," Achin says.

But some proponents of advanced analytics aren't so sure about the ongoing role for humans in complex decision-making processes. The whole point of machine learning is automating the learning process itself, enabling the computer program to get better as it consumes more data, without requiring the continual intervention of a programmer.

"I see a Maslow-type pyramid with BI at the bottom. Above that is human correlation. The next level up is data mining, and the next level after that is predictive analytics. At the peak of the pyramid are the closed-loop systems," says Ravi. "The closed-loop systems aren't telling you what happened, or why something happened, or even what's likely to happen. They're deciding what *should* happen. They're actually making decisions."

As you ascend up the pyramid shown in Figure 10-3, the data management techniques become increasingly action-oriented and more fully automated. At the peak of the pyramid, data management blends seamlessly into decisioning. A use case example from the top of the pyramid is a driverless car, which not only makes decisions in

2 *http://bit.ly/1p6dlE2*

real time without inputs from a human driver, but also gets better with each trip.

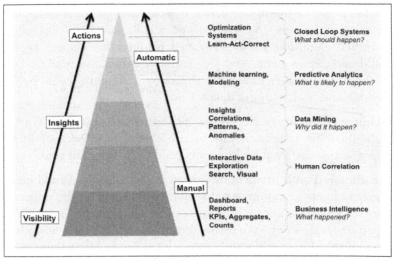

Figure 10-3. Data management hierarchy, visualized as Maslow-type pyramid. Source: T.M. Ravi.

Whether you believe that driverless cars are a great idea or another step toward some kind of dystopian techno-fascism, they certainly illustrate the potential economic value of advanced analytics. Morgan Stanley estimates that self-driving vehicles could save $1.3 trillion annually in the US and $5.6 billion annually worldwide. According to a recent post in RobotEnomics (*http://bit.ly/1sYV8sW*), "the societal and economic benefits of autonomous vehicles include decreased crashes, decreased loss of life, increased mobility for the elderly, disabled, and blind, and decreases in fuel usage."

As cited in the post, Morgan Stanley lists five key areas where the cost savings will come from: "$158 billion in fuel cost savings, $488 billion in annual savings will come through a reduction of accident costs, $507 billion is likely to be gained through increased productivity, reducing congestion will add a further $11 billion in savings, plus an additional $138 billion in productivity savings from less congestion."

The sheer economics of driverless car technology will outweigh other considerations and drive its adoption "sooner than we think," according to the financial services giant.

Transcending Data

Will creating increasingly specialized analytics result in greater "democratization" and wider usage? While that might seem paradoxical, it fits a time-tested pattern: when you make something more relevant and easier to use, more people will use it.

"The last mile is about time-to-value," says Erhardt. "It's about lowering barriers and reducing friction for companies that need to use advanced analytics, but don't have millions of dollars to spend or years to invest in development."

Wise.io, he noted, was founded by people with backgrounds in astronomy. Today, they are working to solve common problems in customer service. "There are still people at some machine learning companies who think their customers are other people with doctoral degrees," he says. "There's nothing wrong with that, but it's a very limited market. We're aiming to help people who don't necessarily have advanced degrees or millions of dollars get started and begin using advanced analytics to help their business."

It seems clear that the world is heading toward greater use of analytics, and that the consumerization of analytics has only just begun. Every step in the evolution of computers and their related systems—from mainframes to client-servers to PCs to mobile devices—was accompanied by a sharp rise in usage. There's no reason to suspect that analytics won't follow a similar trajectory.

"There are only a small number of people in the world with deep experience in machine learning algorithms," says Carlos Guestrin, Amazon professor of machine learning in computer science and engineering at the University of Washington. He is also a cofounder and CEO of Dato (formerly GraphLab), a company focused on large-scale machine learning and graph analytics. "But there is a much wider range of people who want to use machine learning and accomplish super-creative things with it."

Dato provides a relatively simple way for people to write code that runs at scale on Hadoop or EC2 clusters. "The idea here is going from prototype to production or from modeling to deployment very easily," says Guestrin. "Our goal is bringing machine learning to everyone, helping people make the leap from the theoretical to the practical quickly."

For Guestrin, the "last mile of analytics" bridges what he describes as a "usability gap" between hardcore data science and practical applications. He sees himself and other machine learning pioneers as part of a continuum stretching back to the dawn of modern science. "Newton, Kepler, Tycho Brahe, Galileo, and Copernicus— each of them made important contributions based on earlier discoveries. We build on top of existing foundations," Guestrin says, echoing Newton's famous remark, "If I have seen further, it is by standing on the shoulders of giants."

Guestrin and his colleagues aren't exactly comparing themselves to Newton, but it's clear they feel a sense of elation and joy at the prospect of ushering in a new era of advanced analytics.

"Aggregate statistics are about summarizing data. We're already very good at doing that. But the last mile is about transcending data, going beyond it, and making predictions about what's likely to happen next. That's the last mile," he says.

About the Author

Mike Barlow is an award-winning journalist, author, and communications strategy consultant. Since launching his own firm, Cumulus Partners, he has represented major organizations in numerous industries.

Mike is coauthor of *The Executive's Guide to Enterprise Social Media Strategy* (Wiley, 2011) and *Partnering with the CIO: The Future of IT Sales Seen Through the Eyes of Key Decision Makers* (Wiley, 2007). He is also the writer of many articles, reports, and white papers on marketing strategy, marketing automation, customer intelligence, business performance management, collaborative social networking, cloud computing, and big data analytics.

Over the course of a long career, Mike was a reporter and editor at several respected suburban daily newspapers, including *The Journal-News* and the *Stamford Advocate*. His feature stories and columns appeared regularly in *The Los Angeles Times, Chicago Tribune, Miami Herald, Newsday,* and other major US dailies.

Mike is a graduate of Hamilton College. He is a licensed private pilot, an avid reader, and an enthusiastic ice hockey fan. Mike lives in Fairfield, Connecticut, with his wife and their two children.

Colophon

The cover fonts are URW Typewriter and Guardian Sans. The text font is Adobe Minion Pro; the heading font is Adobe Myriad Condensed; and the code font is Dalton Maag's Ubuntu Mono.

Have it your way.

Get even more for your money.

Join the O'Reilly Community, and register the O'Reilly books you own. It's free, and you'll get:

- $4.99 ebook upgrade offer
- 40% upgrade offer on O'Reilly print books
- Membership discounts on books and events
- Free lifetime updates to ebooks and videos
- Multiple ebook formats, DRM FREE
- Participation in the O'Reilly community
- Newsletters
- Account management
- 100% Satisfaction Guarantee

Signing up is easy:

1. Go to: oreilly.com/go/register
2. Create an O'Reilly login.
3. Provide your address.
4. Register your books.

Note: English-language books only

To order books online:
oreilly.com/store

For questions about products or an order:
orders@oreilly.com

To sign up to get topic-specific email announcements and/or news about upcoming books, conferences, special offers, and new technologies:
elists@oreilly.com

For technical questions about book content:
booktech@oreilly.com

To submit new book proposals to our editors:
proposals@oreilly.com

O'Reilly books are available in multiple DRM-free ebook formats. For more information:
oreilly.com/ebooks

CPSIA information can be obtained at www.ICGtesting.com
Printed in the USA
BVOW06s1750021115

425143BV00002B/2/P